Life and Teachings of Ādi Śaṅkarācārya

Andhra University Philosophical Studies, no. 1

Life and Teachings of Ādi Śaṅkarācārya

by

P. George Victor
Professor of Philosophy and Director
Centre for Religious Studies, Andhra University

D.K. Printworld (P) Ltd.
New Delhi

Cataloging in Publication Data — DK

Victor, P. George (Pasalapudi George), 1953–
Life and teachings of Ādi Śaṅkarācārya.
(Andhra University philosophical studies; no. 1).
Includes bibliographical references (p.)
Includes index.

1. Śaṅkarācārya. 2. Hindu philosophers — India — Biography. 3. Philosophy, Hindu. 4. Advaita. I. Title. II. Series: Andha University philosophical studies; no. 1.

ISBN 13 : 978-81-246-0194-5 (HB) ISBN 10 : 81-246-0194-1
ISBN 13 : 978-81-246-0407-6 (PB) ISBN 10 : 81-246-0407-X

First published in India in 2002
Second impression in 2008

Published and printed by:
D.K. Printworld (P) Ltd.
Regd. office: *'Sri Kunj,'* F-52, Bali Nagar
Ramesh Nagar Metro Station
New Delhi - 110 015
Phones : (011) 2545 3975, 2546 6019; *Fax* : (011) 2546 5926
E-mail : dkprintworld@vsnl.net
Web : www.dkprintworld.com

Preface

THIS monograph on Śaṅkarācārya, the great commentator (*bhāṣyakāra*) and theologian of Vedānta, has been the outcome of my post-doctoral research and classroom teaching for post-graduate students in Andhra University.

After the retirement of Professor K. Satchidananda Murty in 1984, I started teaching Śāṅkara Vedānta. As a part of instruction, reading material on Śaṅkara was prepared; thus, the seeds for writing a book on Śaṅkara sowed. I had also the privilege of attending the 'International Seminar on Sankaracarya' held in New Delhi from 9 to 12 January 1989. After listening to the deliberations, I felt that there is a need and scope to write a comprehensive book on the life and teachings of Śaṅkarācārya. Subsequently Prof. K. Satchidananda Murty encouraged me through his letter dated 2 May 1989:

> Dr. Victor . . . if you decide to write a book on Sankara, devote yourself to his Philosophy only. Do not bother about his date and life, because there is no unanimity about them. I wish you to be active and creative, and in due course become well known.

This work took twelve years to complete, as I was sick, once due to handling the old books in the library and later upset due to the death of my father on 14 December 1992. Further, I was also busy as UGC Coordinator, Andhra University from December 1994 to May 1998, Head, Department of Philosophy from July 1995 to June 1998, and Coordinator, UGC Special Assistance Programme, Department of Philosophy, Andhra University from January 1996 to December 2000. At last, I could complete in accordance with the end of UGC Special Assistance Programme.

This book is intended for scholars, students and general readers. Accordingly, the early researches on the date and works of Śaṅkara have been brought out in detail. Not only Śaṅkara's commentaries on the Upaniṣads, *Bhagavad Gītā* and the *Brahma Sūtra* but also the books attributed to him, especially the minor works (*prakaraṇa grantha*s) and hymns (*stotra*s), have been narrated purposefully for the sake of students and general readers. There are certain chapters on the times, method, and social philosophy of Śaṅkara, which were discussed for the first time. Apart from analysing the Vedantic concepts, how the academicians have estimated Śaṅkara has also been added. As a whole, extensive discussion is avoided; precision maintained; the language made simple and the topics are accurate. Though compact, the book is comprehensive in bringing together what the world-teacher (*jagad guru*) has said about Vedānta, the sole message of India.

A study of the commentaries of Śaṅkara and his minor works prove the fact that what Śaṅkara contributed to Indian tradition is not philosophy but theology (*brahma-vidyā*). Prof. K. Satchidananda Murty has also stated that what Śaṅkarācārya has done to Vedic religion, was done by St. Thomas Aquinas to Christianity. Śaṅkarācārya and Thomas Aquinas were more theologians than philosophers. Further the reader is advised that the word 'Brahma' is more appropriate than 'Brahman' to indicate the Absolute God, as the word 'Brahma' was recorded in original Sanskrit works more than the word 'Brahman', appeared in the translations made available in south India.

I acknowledge my indebtedness to the distinguished scholars — Duncan Greenless, Alladi Mahadeva Sastry, S. Radhakrishnan, K.A. Nilakanta Sastry, T.M.P. Mahadevan, Karl H. Potter, K.M. Panikkar, Swami Madhavananda and Swami Gambhirananda, whose works helped me to formulate the content of this book. My association with Prof. S.S. Rama Rao, Pappu, since his organisation of the seminar on 'Perspectives of Vedanta' at Miami

University in 1985 and participation in various sessions of the International Congress of Vedanta, have inspired me to carry out this work. Prof. R. Puligandla, Toledo University, has made positive remarks on the methodology of Śaṅkara. Prof. J.P. Sukla, Former Chairman, Indian Philosophical Congress, Prof. T.S. Devadoss, Madras University, Prof. B. Sambasiva Prasad, Sri Venkateswara University and Dr. S. Penchalaiah, Dravidian University have helped me in various ways, to whom I thank profusely.

I am indebted to the former Vice-Chancellor, Dr. M. Gopalakrishna Reddy for his generous attitude towards my proposals and help extended to carry out various activities in the Department of Philosophy. I wish to thank all my colleagues in the Department of Philosophy, Andhra University, especially to Dr. S.D.A. Joga Rao for his suggestions and corrections in the presswork. This work on Śaṅkarācārya would not have been completed without the love and peace provided by my wife Esther and my children Pranav Raja, Anurag Jose and Shiny Niharika.

My thanks are due to Shri Susheel K. Mittal, Director, D.K. Printworld (P) Ltd. for undertaking the publication and the editorial staff for including the diacritical marks.

P. George Victor
Director
Centre for Religious Studies, and
Professor and Co-ordinator
U.G.C. Special Assistance Programme
Department of Philosophy
Andhra University,
Visakhapatnam - 530 003

To

my father's elder brother

pedda ayya

P. Raja Ratnam

for his enduring love

Contents

	Preface	v
1.	**Introduction to Vedānta**	**1**
	Study of Indian Literature	1
	What are Veda and Vedānta?	3
	The Triple Texts — Prasthānatrayī	4
	The Three Schools	6
	Advaita Vedānta and Indian Mind	7
2.	**Gauḍapāda, the Propounder**	**11**
	The Māṇḍukya Upaniṣad	12
	The Māṇḍukya Kārika	14
	Āgama Prakaraṇa (Chapter on Scripture)	14
	Vaitathya Prakaraṇa (Chapter on unreality)	15
	Advaita Prakaraṇa (Chapter on Non-Duality)	16
	Alātaśānti Prakaraṇa (Chapter on Cerssation of Burning Coal)	17
3.	**The Date of Śaṅkarācārya**	**19**
	The Indian Antiquary	19
	K.B. Pathak — The Source First Discovered	20
	K.T. Telang Rejects K.B. Pathak's Evidence	21
	Telang Rejects Max-Müller's Opinion	22
	Telang Proposes Different Date	23
	W. Logan's Account from Keralotpatti — Date known to Śāṅkara's Native land	26
	D.R. Bhandarkar Supports K.B. Pathak	27

Narasimhachar Exchanges Views with Bhandarkar 28
S.V. Venkateswaran Assigns Śāṅkara to ninth century AD. 29
Conclusion 30

4. **The Times of Śaṅkarācārya** **31**

Political and Social Conditions 32
Religious Conditions 33

5. **The Life of Śaṅkarācārya** **37**

Sources 38
Life at Glance 39
Encounter with an Outcast 40
Religious Harmony and Travels 42

6. **The Works of Śaṅkarācārya** **45**

Paul Hacker's Studies 46
What is His Name? And Which is the Title 47
Works Attributed to Śaṅkarācārya 49

7. **Śaṅkarācārya on the Upaniṣads** **53**

Yājñavalkya and Maitreyī Dialogue 53
Text Summary 53
Śaṅkarācārya's commentary 55
Yājñavalkya and Gārgi Dialogue 57
Text Summary 57
Yājñavalkya Answers the Questions 58
Yājñavalkya Answers Gārgī 59
Śaṅkarācārya's Commentary 59

8. **Śaṅkarācārya on the Bhagavad Gītā** **63**

Introduction 63
Concepts of the Gītā 64
Lord Kṛṣṇa 64
Man 64

Niṣkāma-Karma-yoga 65
Paths of the Gītā 65
Karma-yoga (The Discipline of Action) 65
Jñāna-yoga (The Discipline of Knowledge) 66
Bhakti-yoga (The Discipline of Devotion) 66
Yoga (The Discipline of Meditation) 66
Kṣetra and Kṣetrajña 67
Context 67
Commentary 68
Abandonment and Seeking the Lord as Shelter 72
Commentary 72

9. **Śaṅkarācārya on the Brahma-sūtra** **77**

Bādarāyaṇa 77
Samanvaya (Reconciliation of different statements) 78
Avirodha (Opponent's views criticised) 78
Sādhana (Means) 79
Phala (Fruit, Result) 79
Superimposition (Adhyāsa) 80
The first Brahma Sūtra 83
The Second Brahma Sūtra 85
The Third Brahma Sūtra 87
The Fourth Brahma Sūtra 88
Scriptures are Essential 90
Brahman-knowledge and Mokṣa 91
Seeker of Brahman 93

10. **Minor Works and Hymns of Śaṅkarācārya** **97**

Viveka-cūḍāmaṇi 98
Upadeśa-sahasrī 101
Ātma-bodha 103
Dakṣiṇa-mūrti-stotra 106
Śivānanda-laharī 108
Bhaja-Govindam 110

11.	**Teachings of Śaṅkarācārya**	**113**
	Scripture, Perception and Inference	113
	Brahman-ātman	118
	Brahman and Īśvara	119
	Māyā and World	121
	Jñāna Mārga and Karma Mārga (Path of knowledge and path of Action)	124
	Vyāvahārika-Satya and Pāramārthika Satya (Phenomenal Truth and Noumenal Truth)	127
	Mokṣa	128
12.	**Methodology of Śaṅkarācārya**	**131**
	Scripture as Standard (Śāstra as Pramāṇa)	131
	Writing Commentaries	134
	Missionary Travels	135
	Rejection of Opponent Views	135
	The Dualist	136
	Parables	137
13.	**Social Philosophy of Śaṅkarācārya**	**139**
	Doctrine of Illusion (Māyā-Vāda) — Refuted	139
	Social Order	142
	Ethics	146
14.	**Interpretations on Śāṅkarācārya**	**151**
	Devotional Aspects	152
	Active Social Work	156
	Glossary	161
	Bibliography	165
	Index	169

1

Introduction to Vedānta

RELIGIOUS literature was documented in India from the oldest times of human history. As per the historical evidences, the literary activity in India has not started with written form but orally transmitted. The reasons for oral transmission were that the sacred knowledge of the Vedas, etc., should be given either to a son or to a faithful and disciplined disciple. The Brāhmaṇical law books also emphasised that śūdras should not read and hear the scriptures. Thus, scriptures and works of sages and poets were limited to discipleship but not intended for public.

Apart from oral transmission, manuscripts were written on palm-leaves and strips of birch-bark in later times. The manus cripts were preserved in the private houses of brāhmaṇa *paṇḍit*s, monasteries of Buddhist monks, temples and in the palaces of kings. The oldest Indian manuscripts were found not only in India but also in Nepal, Japan, and Eastern Turkey and in various parts of Asia like Kashgar and Takamakan near Khoṭan. The script used in the ancient literature was Devanāgarī in north India and regional dialects in south India. However, on the basis of vast manuscripts in Sanskrit language, it is generally stated that ancient Indian literature was nothing but Sanskrit literature.

Study of Indian literature

In 1640 the son of Shah Jehan and the brother of Aurangazeb, Prince Dara Shikoh has translated some Upaniṣads into Persian. During the seventeenth and eighteenth centuries some European travellers and missionaries started translating and publishing certain manuscripts. The first Sanskrit book translated into a European language was the *Bhagavad Gītā*. In 1785 Charles Wilkins has translated it into English. He was the first English man who learned the Sanskrit. Later William Jones has published the translations of the *Abhijñānaśākuntalam* of Kālidāsa in 1791 and the law book of Manu in 1794. Henry Thomas Colebrooke (1765-1837), who worked with William Jones, was the actual pioneer for translation of the philosophical and religious literature in India. At the age of 17, H.T. Colebrooke came to India in 1782 and devoted his entire life to the study and translation of Vedic texts. His essays on the Vedas and different systems of Indian thought which were published in 1837 as a book became model for the later historians of Indian philosophy. It was an outcome of 40 years of research. In 1784 the Asiatic Society of Bengal was established to collect the various manuscripts. H.T. Colebrooke was appointed as its President in 1807.

Different men from various parts of the country procured the manuscripts of the Vedas. In 1805 H.T. Colebrooke wrote in the *Asiatic Researches* about the efforts the early researchers have made:

> In the early progress of researches into Indian literature, it was doubted whether the Vedas were extant or preserved. . . . The doubts were not finally abandoned, until Colonel Polier obtained from Jeypur a transcript of what purported to be a complete copy of the Vedas, and which he deposited in the British Museum. About the same time Sir Robert Chambers collected at Benaras numerous fragments of the Indian Scripture. General Martine, at a later period, obtained copies of some parts of it; and Sir William Jones was successful in procuring valuable portions of the Vedas, and in translating several curious passages from one of them. I have been still more fortunate in collecting at Benaras the text and commentary of a large portion of these celebrated books.[1]

---

1. H.T. Colebrooke, *Essays on the Religion and Philosophy of the Hindus*, 1976, p. 1.

In the early forties of the nineteenth century, a Vedic scholar and French Orientalist Eugen Burnouf laid the foundation for the study of Vedas in Europe. Later his pupils like Rudolph Roth and F. Max-Müller started publishing the hymns of the Vedas. No book of the Vedas was published until 1839, except the first and eighth parts of the *R̥gveda* by Frederic Rosen.

What are Veda and Vedānta?

The word *Veda* means 'knowledge that is sacred and religious'. The Vedas are four in number: *R̥gveda*, *Sāmaveda*, *Yajurveda* and *Atharvaveda*. Manu and other authors of law books have mentioned only the first three Vedas. However the Upaniṣads and Purāṇas recorded and also the Vedic tradition included the fourth Veda. Generally each Veda is divided into four parts. H.T. Colebrooke and S.N. Dasgupta have considered this division. The first part of each Veda is *Saṁhitā* or collection of verses. The second is the *Brāhmaṇa*s and third is the *Āraṇyaka*s that form the religious and forest treatises dealing with rituals and worship. The fourth part of each Veda or the concluding portions are the Upaniṣads, those contain various sorts of theological discussions and utterances of truths perceived by the sages.

The Vedas were written in the archaic Sanskrit that differs from the classical Sanskrit. The classical Sanskrit is that which is in accordance with the rules of Pāṇini's grammar that flourished in the fifth century BC among the elite and the courts of kings. The Vedic literature is a collection of songs and prayer books, theological and theosophical treatises. They represent a unity, and form the basis for the Brāhmaṇical religious life. The content and the knowledge of the Vedas were revealed to the ancient sages and therefore, human authorship was denied, they were *apauruṣeya*.

The concluding portions of the Vedas are Upaniṣads; and therefore, the thought of the Upaniṣads is 'Vedānta'. The Upaniṣads have influenced the Indian thinkers from the earliest times onwards and represent the culmination of Indian thought. In the later period, the *Brahma Sūtra* and the *Bhagavad Gītā* have become the source books of Vedānta along with the Upaniṣads. To this extent, the exponents of different schools of Vedānta drew their inspiration and interpretation from these scriptures.

Vedānta is also known as Uttara-Mīmāṁsā as the word *mīmāṁsā* actually means 'solution of problems by reflection and critical examination'. There is Pūrva-Mīmāṁsā, which justifies Vedic rituals considering the older portions of the Vedas faithfully and also the Uttara-Mīmāṁsā that interprets the later portions of the Vedas, called Upaniṣads. H.T. Colebrooke writes that Pūrva-Mīmāṁsā explains the practical part of the Vedas, while the Uttara-Mīmāṁsā represents the theological part of the Vedas.[2] Similarly Paul Deussen remarks that the Pūrva-Mīmāṁsā and the Uttara-Mīmāṁsā constitutes the whole philosophy of Vedas like the Old and New Testaments of the *Bible*.[3] The Pūrva-Mīmāṁsā and Uttara-Mīmāṁsā constitute the *karma-kāṇḍa and jñāna-kāṇḍa* portions of the Vedas respectively.

The triple texts — prasthānatrayī

Traditionally scholars call the Upaniṣads, the *Brahma Sūtra* and the *Bhagavad Gītā* as *prasthānatrayī*, but it actually means 'the triple great ways' probably meant the three schools that formulate the foundation of the Vedānta Philosophy.

The word *upaniṣad* indicates 'sacred or secret instruction' as mentioned in the Upaniṣads. The etymological meaning of it is 'sitting down near a teacher and listening to him'. During the seventeenth century, Prince Dara Shikoh, as stated by H.T. Colebrooke has collected 50 Upaniṣads. In 1917 the Nirnaya Sagar Press in Bombay has published 102 Upaniṣads. The *Muktika Upaniṣad* had mentioned 108 Upaniṣads. Among these Upaniṣads, Śaṅkarācārya, the great exponent of Advaita Vedānta, has considered 10 important Upaniṣads and commented upon them. They are *Īśa*, *Kena*, *Kaṭha*, *Praśna*, *Muṇḍaka*, *Māṇḍūkya*,

---

2. H.T. Colebrooke, *op.cit.*, p. 208.
3. Paul Deussen, *The System of Vedānta*, 1972, p. 20.

Aitareya, *Taittirīya*, *Chāndogya* and *Bṛhadāraṇyaka* Upaniṣads. In addition to these, scholars of Vedānta consider *Kauṣītaki*, *Śvetāśvatara*, *Mahānārāyaṇa* and *Maitrī* Upaniṣads as important.

Many scholars are of the opinion that these Upaniṣads are composed not at a time but spread over to many centuries before the Christian era. The scholars have placed them to the sixth century BC. Though the Upaniṣads are the ending portions of the Vedas, they differ from the earlier portions in spirit and content. Therefore, the Upaniṣads became popular independently and insist the path of knowledge (*jñāna-mārga*) in opposition to the path of action (*karma-mārga*) as advocated in the Vedas. The Upaniṣads, as a whole, are not systematic philosophical treatises but recorded statements and utterances of truth and reality perceived by the ancient sages of India. They reveal the ancient man's desire to know the Ultimate Truth and the knowledge that emancipates individual from the 'world of suffering' (*saṁsāra*).

The Vedānta thinkers accept the *Bhagavad Gītā* as one of the source books of Vedānta. The *Bhagavad Gītā*, the poem of God, is a part of the great Indian epic, the *Mahābhārata* and contains 700 poems (*śloka*s), divided into 18 chapters. The *Bhagavad Gītā* was a dialogue between Śrī Kṛṣṇa and Arjuna taken place at the war-field, Kurukṣetra; but Sañjaya, who has witnessed the discussion, conveyed the same to king Dhṛtarāṣṭra. Scholars who have critically studied the *Bhagavad Gītā* are of the opinion that it is a post-Buddhist work and formed in the present state during the fourth or third century BC.

Besides the Upaniṣads and the *Bhagavad Gītā*, the *Brahma Sūtra* exclusively discusses the doctrines of Vedānta; hence, it is called the *Vedānta-sūtra*s. The *Brahma Sūtra* is a text of 555 aphorisms (*sūtra*s) each consisting three to four words. The *Brahma Sūtra* contains four chapters and each chapter divided into four sections. The author of this *sūtra* is Bādarāyaṇa, who attempted to record the essence of the Upaniṣads in theorems or aphorisms. Therefore, the later thinkers of Vedānta understood it in different ways. Consequently they gave a variety of meanings and interpretations to the aphorisms of Bādarāyaṇa. Thus, the three scriptures are basis for Vedānta representing the *śruti*, *smṛti* and *sūtra* literature.

The three schools

The message of Vedānta was interpreted in three different ways by three great teachers (*ācārya*s) — Śaṅkarācārya, Rāmānujācārya and Madhvācārya. The Vedānta of Śaṅkarācārya is Non-Dual (Advaita) Vedānta or Monism. Śaṅkarācārya interprets that the Supreme Self (*Brahman*) is the sole reality and devoid of all distinctions. The empirical world is in a state of illusion (*māyā*) and the individual self (*ātmā*) is nothing but the Supreme Self (*Brahman*). Further, he says that the nature of the world is illusion (*māyā*). Figuratively speaking, *māyā* is the veil of non-cognition or ignorance that makes a person not to comprehend the reality of the world. Śaṅkarācārya says that liberation (*mokṣa*) is to be attained through the knowledge of *Brahman*.

Rāmānujācārya's interpretation of Vedānta is 'Qualified Non-Dualism' (Viśiṣṭādvaita Vedānta). He says that objects in the world and selves (*jīva*s) are different from *Brahman*. He interprets that *Brahman* possesses certain specific qualities different from self, and the self cannot exist apart from *Brahman*. By interpreting *Brahman* with attributes, Rāmānujācārya affirms devotion (*bhakti*) on the part of the individual to attain liberation (*mokṣa*).

While Śaṅkarācārya discusses *Brahman* in pure abstraction as *nirguṇa* Brahma, Rāmānujācārya maintains *Brahman* as *saguṇa* Brahma (God with good characteristics). He says that *māyā* is the power of *Brahman* but not the illusory nature of the empirical world. Like Śaṅkarācārya, Rāmānujācārya has commented upon the *prasthānatrayī*. In this connection, George Theibaut is of the opinion that Rāmānujācārya's commentary is most faithful to the *Brahma Sūtra* than the commentary of Śaṅkarācārya.

The other commentator of Vedānta, Madhva propounded the

Dualism (Dvaita Vedānta). According to him, the world is different from *Brahman*, likewise the individual self (*ātma*). Madhva says that though the objects in the world change from time to time, they are real; and liberation (*mokṣa*) comes to devotee by the grace of God, *Brahman*. Thus Madhva affirms reality as well as distinction of the objects, world and self from *Brahman*.

Advaita Vedānta and Indian mind

Vedānta is the leading philosophy of Vedic tradition and its view of life dominated the Indian Mind for centuries. With its emphasis on the unperceived reality of the world, the place of man in it and with the notions of *māyā* and *saṁsāra*, Vedānta has influenced the elite and folk equally through the literature of teachers and songs of saints. Various factors and conditions contributed for the wider acceptance of Vedāntic view would be as follows:

1. The term *vedānta* is the etymological extension of the Veda and shows the continuation of the Veda; and Vedic tradition in India being the established religion naturally perpetuated the Vedāntic view.

2. Vedānta notions of *Brahman*, world, transmigration and *māyā* do find similarities in the sayings and messages of poets and sages of all cults and creeds in India.

3. Vedāntic is popular because of its stress on the path of knowledge (*jñāna-kāṇḍa*) which can be followed by poor *paṇḍit*s and disciplined persons when compared to the path of practice (*karma-kāṇḍa*) which requires wealth, time and co-ordination of actions and persons.

4. The educated Indians, who did not generally show interest in mundane exercises, were attracted by Vedānta as it gives them solace through mere reading, studying and understanding the scripture.

5. The various interpretations given by the great teachers in the middle ages sustained and helped for the growth and continuation of Vedānta.

6. The Upaniṣads and the *Bhagavad Gītā*, as the fundamental books have advocated and advanced ethics and principles those minimise the antagonism among the various social groups of India. This made the masses to appreciate the central doctrines of Vedānta texts against the social antagonism prevailed in the society.
7. Vedānta provides the modern Hindu, the required and aspired religion of high order compatible to Christianity and Islam.
8. Vedānta apart from Vedic religion provides the theological aspect for the spiritual desire of individuals; thus it is different from a number of cults and religious rituals prevailed among different regions of India.
9. Vedānta stands alone as a pure theological school that differs with in ritual methods, mundane world, logical disputations and abstract analysis of objective world as found in other systems of Indian philosophy.

Thus Vedānta has become a religion, philosophy and theology of the educated and elite modern Hindu. In the modern times Vedānta became a missionary religion, and the educated Indian understands it through the interpretations made available by the Rāmakr̥ṣṇa Mission. The Rāmakr̥ṣṇa Mission established by Swāmī Vivekānanda has taken up the publication of Vedānta texts and the translation of the commentaries of Śaṅkarācārya. This missionary zeal has touched the educated Indian and poured in him the glorious tradition of India with the Vedāntic spirit. Thus Vedānta became synonymous to Advaita Vedānta of Śaṅkarācārya.

In brief, Śaṅkarācārya has laid the foundation for the propagation of Vedānta before the beginning of middle ages; and it was nourished by Rāmakr̥ṣṇa Mission and Swāmī Vivekānanda in the modern period and in the contemporary period Radhakrishnan and other academic teachers have contributed for its bloom.[4] Swāmī Vivekānanda has appraised the Advaita aspect of Vedānta on the ground that it advocates the identity of man and God, and the equal status of every individual. In his hands the Vedānta has become 'Practical Vedānta', an ideology for social emancipation of the śūdras, women and untouchables. Subsequently, Radhakrishnan interpreted it as a place of resort for all differences, disputes and international problems. He perceived it as a way that puts an end to the crisis of national and international issues and disputes of religious and secular nature; and the same is found in his books. Thus, Vedānta, especially the Advaita Vedānta, has dominated the Indian Mind.

4. Hiltrud Rustau has explained in terms of historical necessity, the evolution and development of Śāṅkara Vedānta in her article, 'The Place of Śaṅkara in Indian Philosophy and his influence on Modern Indian Thinkers', *vide* R. Balasubramanian and Sibajivan Bhattacharya, ed., *Perspectives of Śaṅkara*, 1989, pp. 381-92.

2

Gauḍapāda, the Propounder

GAUḌAPĀDA is the propounder of Advaita Vedānta. In the hands of Śaṅkarācārya, Advaita Vedānta became a school of thought with a laborious literary work and missionary zeal of propagation. Ānandagiri, in his *ṭīkā* (glossary) on the *Māṇḍūkya-Kārikā-Bhāṣya* mentions that Gauḍapāda lived in the Badrikāśrama. It was also mentioned by scholars that due to the curse of Patañjali, Gauḍapāda become a *brahma-rākṣasa* (great devil) for some time and lived on a tree at the bank of river Narmadā.[1]

Gauḍapāda wrote a verse commentary (*kārikā*) on the *Māṇḍūkya Upaniṣad.* The other works attributed to Gauḍapāda are *Uttara-Bhagavad-Gītā-Vṛtti*, *Sāṁkhya-Kārikā-Bhāṣya*, *Durgāsaptaśatī-Bhāṣya*, *Nṛsiṁhottara-tapinyopaniṣad-Bhāṣya*, *Subhāgodaya* and *Śrīvidyāratna-Sūtra*. There is no authoritative evidence for his authorship of these works except his *Māṇḍūkya Kārikā*, which laid the foundations for Advaita. Gauḍapāda was teacher to Govinda, Śaṅkarācārya's teacher. This is confirmed on the basis of a verse that describes the list of teachers.[2] Though the monistic-view (Advaita) was recorded in the Upaniṣads, but Gauḍapāda explained it systematically in his *kārikā* on the *Māṇḍūkya Upaniṣad*.

Govinda was a brāhmaṇa of Kaśmīr and in his earlier stage

---

1. More details on the date and identity of Gauḍapāda are found in T.M.P. Mahadevan, *Gauḍapāda: A Study in Early Advaita*, 1960, pp. 1-15.
2. *Ibid.*, p. 2.

of life his name was Candra Śarmā. While he was coming to the south India, on the banks of river Narmadā he happened to meet Gauḍapāda and learned grammar (*vyākaraṇa*) for nine days non-stop. Govinda has taken the teaching on the leaves of a tree using his blood as ink as there were no writing instruments. Later Govinda returned to the Badrikāśrama and became a *saṁnyāsin*. Again Govinda took up his journey to the south, and on the banks of river Narmadā he accepted Śaṅkarācārya as his disciple and initiated him in all the great sentences (*mahāvākya*s).

The life of Govinda is associated with a romantic story. While he was going to Badrikāśrama on the way at Ujjain he became unconscious on the pile of a merchant (vaiśya). The daughter of the merchant saved him and her father requested Govinda to marry his daughter. When Govinda refused, the merchant took him to the court of the king. The king delighted with the beauty of Govinda and thought of giving his daughter in marriage. He consulted the brāhmaṇa minister about the sanction of the law for such a marriage. As the minister had also a daughter he wanted to give his daughter. Consequently Govinda married all the three girls and stayed with them until each one of them had a son by him. Later in Badrikāśrama, he became a *saṁnyāsin* and known as Govinda.[3]

The Māṇḍūkya Upaniṣad

The *Māṇḍūkya Upaniṣad* contains 12 verses relating to the fundamental issues of self and world. The first verse of this Upaniṣad starts with the syllable *oṁ* and concludes that whosoever realises *oṁ* as *ātma* attains the Supreme Self, *Brahman*. The essence and message of the *Māṇḍūkya Upaniṣad* are:

> *Oṁ* is the whole world,
> the past, the present, the future, everything is
> just the word *oṁ*.

---

3. Govinda in earlier life-stage as Candra Śarmā was discussed by V.A. Devasenāpati in his article 'Govinda Bhagavadpāda' in T.M.P. Mahadevan, ed., *The Preceptor's of Advaita*, 1968, pp. 43-6.

For truly, everything here is *Brahman*;
this self (*ātma*) is *Brahman*.[4]

The *Māṇḍūkya Upaniṣad* describes that the self has four states (*sthānas*):

1. The waking state (*jāgr̥ta sthāna*); 2. The dreaming state (*svapna sthāna*); 3. The deep-sleep state (*suṣupta sthāna*); 4. The fourth state (*caturtha sthāna*).

1. The waking state is common to all people. In this state, the self (*ātma*) enjoys life with the five organs of senses (*buddhi indriyas*) hearing, sense, sight, taste and smell with their actions (*karma indriyas*), wherein mind (*manas*) intellect (*buddhi*) egoism (*ahaṁkāra*) and thinking (*citta*) acts upon.
2. In the dreaming state also all the senses and the activities of the self will continue but possesses a kind of extra brilliance while inwardly cognitive and being in sleep.
3. In the deep-sleep state the self becomes a cognitive-mass (*prajñāna-ghana*) with consisting bliss (*ānanda-maya*) and enjoining-bliss (*ānanda-bhuja*). It is lord of all (*sarveśvara*), all knowing (*sarvajña*), inner-controller (*antaryāmin*) and source (*yoni*) of all.
4. The fourth state has been described in other Upaniṣads as *turīya*, which is the state of being one with the self (*ekātmya pratyaya sāra*) and the state of being 'free from the world' (*prapañca upasama*) by attaining tranquil (*śānta*) and benign (Śiva) without a second (Advaita).[5]

---

4. *Māṇḍūkya Upaniṣad*, 2. Cf., R.E. Hume, *The Thirteen Principal Upaniṣads*, 1949, p. 391.
5. *Ibid*., p. 392.

The Māṇḍūkya Kārikā[6]

The *Māṇḍūkya Kārikā* of Gauḍapāda explains elaborately the self and world, because the experiences and states (*sthānas*) of the self are being either outwardly or inwardly related to the world. The *kārikā* is not a commentary in the strict sense, but a precise verse commentary on the *Māṇḍūkya Upaniṣad* containing 215 verses written for the sake of remembering the doctrines. The *Māṇḍūkya Kārikā* consists of four chapters (*prakaraṇas*):

1. *Āgama Prakaraṇa*, containing 29 verses.
2. *Vaitathya Prakaraṇa*, containing 38 verses.
3. *Advaita Prakaraṇa*, containing 48 verses.
4. *Alataśānti Prakaraṇa*, containing 100 verses.

ĀGAMA PRAKARAṆA (CHAPTER ON SCRIPTURE)

In this chapter Gauḍapāda explains the three states of the self as the *vaiśvānara ātma*, *taijasa ātma*, *prajñāna ātma*. He remarks that in the fourth state, the self (*ātmā*) cannot be explained. In this context he discussed the theories of creation (*sṛṣṭi*). The world, he says, is a result or expansion (*vibhūti*), it is like a dream (*svapna*), a play (*krīḍā*) of God, and it is for enjoyment (*bhoga*) of God. This chapter contains all that analysed in the *Māṇḍūkya Upaniṣad*, thus the *kārikā* is a supplementary verse-commentary on the Upaniṣad. Further Gauḍapāda says that all beings, those created have only life breath (*prāṇa*) while the humans (*puruṣa*) have consciousness. Gauḍapāda in this context says:

> Dream belongs to one who sees falsely,
> And sleep to one who does not know Reality.
> When the two errors of these two are removed,
> One attains the state, that is *turīya*[7]

---

6. Swāmī Gambhīrānanda's translation of the *Māṇḍūkya-Kārikā* is precise and accurate of all the available works avoiding the complicated later commentaries. All the quotations hereafter on the *Māṇḍūkya-Kārikā, Kena, Praśna, Muṇḍaka and Taittirīya Upaniṣad Bhāṣyas* are from Swāmī Gambhīrānanda, tr., *Eight Upaniṣads*, 1978.

7. *Māṇḍūkya-Kārikā*, I.15, in *Eight Upaniṣads*,vol. 2, p. 216.

VAITATHYA PRAKARAṆA (CHAPTER ON UNREALITY)

Gauḍapāda writes that all-thinking (*sarva-bhāvanā*) in dream is false,[8] because the dreamer does not experience it, when awakened. Therefore the objects are false in the dream state and also in the waking state. In other words, the waking state and the dreaming state are one for the wise. According to Gauḍapāda, whatever those have an origin will necessarily cease.

In the darkness of night, one may consider the rope to be a snake or a line of water.[9] Similarly the self is a vital force (*prāṇa*), element, category, quality and, etc., but in reality it is not. Vedic scholars believe in the reality of the Vedas like the specialists belief in micro-things, physicists believe in physical forms; and astrologers, lawyers, psychologists, intellectuals, philologists and painters believe in their own ways and the reality of what they know. Thus one's own things of pleasure are real for one. Some people believe in the creation, and others in dissolution but some others believe the ways of the world. Gauḍapāda says that the universe (*viśvam*) is like dream-illusion (*svapna-māyā*) city in the sky (*gandharva-nagaram*)[10] and known for those who had discriminative knowledge from the standpoint of Vedānta. Accordingly Swāmī Prabhavānanda observes:

> Consistent with his Philosophy of Non-Dualism, Gauḍapāda did not believe in the absolute reality of creation. The one absolute, non-dual self, or God neither created this universe nor did he become this universe. In reality there is no creation, for the one infinite existence appears to be the manifold universe just as a rope may appear to be a snake. The universe is not a reality but something superimposed upon the *ātma*.[11]

Hence, the highest-truth (*paramārtha*) is that there is no

---

8. *Māṇḍūkya-Kārikā*, II.14, in *Eight Upaniṣads*, vol. 2, p. 232.
9. *Ibid.*, II.17, *ibid.*, p. 246.
10. *Ibid.*, II.31, *ibid.*, p. 255.
11. Swāmī Prabhavānanda, *The Spiritual Heritage of India*, 1977, p. 277.

dissolution and origination of the world. Hence, there shall not be any bondage of the self and a desire for liberation; therefore no one to be liberated. This is the Philosophy (*tattva*) to know, says Gauḍapāda. *Tattvavido* is the word used by Gauḍapāda for referring to 'one who knows the truth', the philosopher. He says that 'Philosophy is metaphysical', *tattvam ādhyātmikam*.[12]

ADVAITA PRAKARAṆA (CHAPTER ON NON-DUALITY)

Self (*ātma*) is just like space in the jar. When the jar broke, the space confined to the jar will disintegrate and merge in the universal space. So is the case for self. Space (*ākāśa*) in different jars is called with different names and forms, yet there is no plurality. The self is same in all bodies like the space. Differences are due to illusion of the self (*ātma-māyā*).[13] Thus Gauḍapāda asserts that 'Highest truth is non-dual', *advaitam paramārtha*.[14]

It seems for Gauḍapāda *māyā* means 'the unknowable'. Accordingly he uses the following terms:

anādi māyayā, 'The ungraspable is beginning less.'
— chapter I, verse 17

māyā mātra midam, 'Here exists the form of unknown.'
— chapter I, verse 18

māyayā bhidyate, 'Plurality is unknown.'
— chapter III, verse 19

māyābhiritya pe, 'The diverse forms cannot be grasped.'
— chapter III, verse 24

māyayā janma, 'Birth is unknown.'
— chapter III, verse 27

According to Gauḍapāda the mind always reflects in dual way, either in dreaming state or waking state. By remembering

12. *Māṇḍūkya-Kārikā*, II.38, in *Eight Upaniṣads*., vol. 2, p. 266.
13. *Ibid.*, II.10, *ibid.*, pp. 280-1.
14. *Ibid.*, III.18, *ibid.*, p. 291.

that all-human effort, desires and enjoyments are full of sorrow that one should withdraw the mind. Mind should be kept with tranquillity, purity and peace; and thus the highest and the happiest (*uttama-sukham*) is the perfect withdrawal (*sa-nirvāṇam*).[15]

ALĀTAŚĀNTI PRAKARAṆA (CHAPTER ON CESSATION OF BURNING COAL)

In this chapter Gauḍapāda advocates discipline of non-attachment (*asparśa yoga*) which seeks the welfare and good comforts of all beyond disputes and controversies.[16] Gauḍapāda writes that even the causation theory of birth and death and related analogies have no relevance at all. In other words, if every effect has a cause, then the cause should have another cause and thus the theory results in unending search. Gauḍapāda argues that it is futile to estimate the relationship between cause and effect and creation. On certain occasions with emotion in the waking state, unreal things will be considered as real similar to the dreaming state. Due to lack of discriminating knowledge, some people believe in unthinkable objects. Therefore Gauḍapāda says that to avoid fear among the ignorant, the doctrine of no-birth and the creation theory have been preached. For Gauḍapāda the creation is like an 'illusory elephant' (*māyā-hasti*).[17]

Gauḍapāda further explains about human thinking (*cintā*). According to him, thinking has no birth, therefore it has no termination and even the souls are birthless.[18] In common experience the movement of the burning coal appears to be straight or curved as per the movement caused.[19] In reality the burning coal moved in the air is neither straight nor curved. Similarly it is so in the case of thinking (*cintā*). Whatever that impressed upon our thinking will not remain. Human thinking

---

15. *Māṇḍūkya-Kārikā*, III.47, in *Eight Upaniṣads*, vol. 2, p. 322.
16. *Ibid.*, IV.2, *ibid.*, p. 326.
17. *Ibid.*, IV. 44, *ibid.*, pp. 362, 363.
18. *Ibid.*, IV.46, *ibid.*, p. 363.
19. *Ibid.*, IV.47, *ibid.*, p. 364.

is not a kind of substance. As per the theory of causation, the world continues as long as one thinks. There is neither beginning nor end; the correct idea or the perfect perspective (*sad- bhāvanā*) is that everything is birth-less (*sarvam-ajam*) and there is no creation.[20] Gauḍapāda writes:

> The entities that are born thus are not born in reality.
> Their birth is as that of a thing through *māyā* (magic).
> And that *māyā* again has no reality.[21]

All creatures appear and disappear in dreams. All objects of perception in dreaming state are real for the dreamer and limited to that consciousness. Similarly all objects of perception in waking state are real to the consciousness of the person in waking state. Thus our experiences are relative with reference to the state. Gauḍapāda says that thinking related to worldly apprehension is of no use. Different theories advocated the existence of the self and non-existence of the self. All the theories do not pertain to the absolute reality.[22] The enlightened persons do not entertain the disputes and remain in tranquillity being unaffected by duality. For the people, who think that souls are born with characteristics and adjuncts do need acquisition of knowledge. According to S.N. Dasgupta, Gauḍapāda has assimilated all the Buddhist *śūnyavāda* teachings, and thought that these held good of the ultimate truth preached by the Upaniṣads.[23]

Radhakrishnan says that not only in doctrines, but also in phraseology, Buddhism has influenced Gauḍapāda. He says that the negative tendency of Gauḍapāda has been met in the hands of Śaṅkarācārya with a balanced outlook.[24]

---

20. *Māṇḍūkya-Kārikā*, IV.57, in *Eight Upaniṣads*, vol. 2, p. 371.
21. *Ibid.*, IV.58, *ibid.*
22. *Ibid.*, IV.83, *ibid.*, p. 387.
23. S.N. Dasgupta, *A History of Indian Philosophy*, vol. I, 1975, p. 429.
24. Radhakrishnan, *Indian Philosophy*, vol. II, 1966, p. 465.

3

The Date of Śaṅkarācārya

It is interesting to note that a good amount of research has been done to know the date of Śaṅkara, though a common agreement has not been evolved. The Śaṅkara monasteries at Dvārakā, Purī and Kāñcī maintain 509 BC as the year of the birth of Śaṅkara, while the Śṛṅgerī monastery states it as 44 BC.

Śaṅkarācārya, in his *Brahma-Sūtra-Bhāṣya*, has mentioned the name of the city of Pāṭaliputra and a name called Pūrṇavarmā. On the basis of these two references a historical discussion has taken place. It is established that the city of Pāṭaliputra was destroyed by river-erosion during AD 750. And the Chinese pilgrim Hiuen Tsang mentioned the name of Pūrṇavarmā who was considered as a Buddhist king of Magadha during AD 590. Thereby some scholars concluded that AD 700 as the beginning of the life of Śaṅkara. H.T. Colebrooke, after discussing with Raja Rammohun Roy, Wilson and some other Sanskrit scholars of his time, writes that Śaṅkara flourished during the close of the eighth or the beginning of the ninth century AD. Max-Müller, Macdonell, Dasgupta, Nilakantha Sastry and many others accepted AD 788-820, as the dates of Śaṅkara. The reason for accepting them is the research involved in confirming them. Necessary doubts have been raised and solved with reference to these dates and they have been published in *The Indian Antiquary*.

The Indian Antiquary

The Indian Antiquary was a journal of oriental research in archaeology, history, literature, languages, folklore, philosophy and religion. The first issue of it was released on 5th January 1872, and Jas Burgess was its founding editor. For about 61 years lasting in 1933, it was published regularly and various scholars and administrators like Jas Burgess, John Faithful Fleet, Richard Carnac Temple, Devadatta Rāmākr̥ṣṇa Bhandarkar, Krishna Swami Aiyangar, Stephen Meradyth Edwards and Charles E.A.W. Oldham have been its editors in succession. It is interesting for researchers that more than 10 volumes of this journal contain studies on Śaṅkarācārya.

Later a second series of it had appeared during 1934-47 with the title *New Indian Antiquary* edited by S.M. Katre and P.K. Gode. In these series the ninth volume, published in 1947 carried a research article on Śaṅkarācārya by Paul Hacker of Germany. Trials have been made for its publication after 20 years in 1969 and G.V. Devasthali had brought out third series entitled *Indian Antiquary*.

The Indian Antiquary has carried the most fascinating discussions over the date of Śaṅkarācārya. In 1882 the editor of it has mentioned for the first time and he writes:

> Prof. Teile (*Outlines of the History of Ancient Religions*, p. 140) had, in 1877, given AD 788 as the date of the birth of Śaṅkara. If he died in S.742 or AD 820-21, he could only have been 32 years of age.[1]

K.B. PATHAK — THE SOURCE FIRST DISCOVERED

For the first time, the June 1882 part of *The Indian Antiquary* carried an informative article by K.B. Pathak, BA, of Belgaum High School. He states:

> I have lately come across a manuscript which gives the date of Śaṅkarācārya. The manuscript belongs to Mr. Govinda Bhatta Yerlekara of Belgaum. It is a small one,

1. *The Indian Antiquary*, vol. XI, 1882, p. 263.

> consisting of three leaves only, written in *Balbodh* Characters.[2]

Then K.B. Pathak stated that it is in Devanāgarī script. P. Sundaram Pillai, while he was discussing the conditions in Kerala at the times of Śaṅkarācārya made the translation of that and writes:

> The only definite date yet assigned to the ācārya with any degree of probability is that of Mr. K.B. Pathak, according to whom Śaṅkara must have died in 820 AD. The date of his birth, according to the *slokas* in a manuscript volume in the possession of one, Govinda Bhatta of Belgaum, is *Vibhava Varṣa*, Kali year 3889; and that of his death, full moon in *Vaiśākha*, Kali year 3921.[3]

K.T. TELANG REJECTS K.B. PATHAK'S EVIDENCE

Kashinath Triambak Telang was a Senior Dakshina Fellow of Elphinston College. He has put forward the following reasons opposing the dates proposed by K.B. Pathak. Telang's arguments are as follows:[4]

1. K.B. Pathak's date of Śaṅkara is accepted from a stanza in a work whose author and his age is not specified. It is said that the work is related to twelfth century AD, which is very later time to the period of Śaṅkara having 350 years of interval. There is no reliable information to find out the value of the materials from which Pathak ascertained the date.

2. Prof. Tiele in his *History of Ancient Religions*, published in 1877 has earlier mentioned this date of Śaṅkara. Therefore, it is evident that K.B. Pathak is not revealing any new thing. In this connection Telang says, that this

---

2. *The Indian Antiquary*, vol. XI, 1882, p. 175.
3. *Ibid.*, vol. XXVI, 1897, p. 117.
4. *Ibid.*, vol. XIII, 1884, pp. 95-103.

information might have gathered from Yagneswara Sastri's *Arya vidya Sudhakara*. According to Telang, Mr. Sastri suggested this date firstly on the basis of a stanza which has come down through the tradition or *sampradaya*; secondly with reference to a stanza found in Bhatta Nilakantha's *Śaṅkara Mandāra Saurabha*.

3. Telang gives another source of the date of Sankara; he states *The Indian Antiquary* vol. III, p. 282 . . . have an extract from the *Keralotpatti* which yields 400 AD as the year of Sankara's birth. It also states that Sankara died when he was 38 years of age.

Therefore, K.T. Telang points out that there was no historical and rational ground to reject the stanzas of *Keralotpatti* and for acceptance of other stanzas those stated by K.B. Pathak.

TELANG REJECTS MAX-MÜLLER'S OPINION

K.T. Telang analyses that Max-Müller has accepted the date proposed by K.B. Pathak without critical outlook. Following are the grounds for his rejection of Max-Müller's opinion:

1. Śaṅkara mentioned in his *Brahma-Sūtra-Bhāṣya*, 2.1.17 the names of Srughna and Pāṭaliputra. It is implied that Śaṅkara lived when these cities were in existence. But historically it is evident that Pāṭaliputra was destroyed by a river inundation about the middle of the eighth century AD or AD 750. Therefore, Śaṅkara must have lived earlier to this date.
2. In the same *Brahma-Sūtra-Bhāṣya* again at 2.1.17, Śaṅkara has mentioned king Pūrṇavarmā. The study of various names of kings ending with the word 'Varmā' of various dynasties reveals that there were two such names. Firstly two inscriptions at Jāvā mentioned the name of Pūrṇavarmā. Secondly, the Buddhist pilgrim from China, Hiuen Tsang has also mentioned.

Hence, Telang argues that Śaṅkara might have referred to this king of Magadha, whom Hiuen Tsang mentioned but not the Pūrṇavarmā of Jāvā, which is a far-east country. Telang substantiates this view with the following points:

(i) Mādhavācārya in his book *Śaṅkara Vijaya* writes that Śaṅkara was at Benāras when he wrote the *Brahma-Sūtra-Bhāṣya*.

(ii) Ānandagiri's *Śaṅkara Vijaya* also contains that Śaṅkara wrote the *Brahma-Sūtra-Bhāṣya* before he left to the south.

(iii) M. Barth in his work, *Religions of India* states that Śaṅkara has not written his *Brahma-Sūtra-Bhāṣya* in the south.

(iv) Śaṅkara has not mentioned anything that is related to the south in his *Brahma-Sūtra-Bhāṣya*.

Therefore, Telang argues that Śaṅkara belongs to the time of king Pūrṇavarmā who reigned Magadha during the end of the sixth century AD.

TELANG PROPOSES DIFFERENT DATE

Telang assigns the date of Śaṅkara to the end of sixth century AD; and he advanced the following six arguments in support of the date:

1. (a) Hiuen Tsang had spent two years 637, 638 in Magadha during the period of his visit to India from AD 629 to 645, though he mentioned the name of king Pūrṇavarmā as the descendant of Aśoka, but he had not made any visit to this Buddhist king.

(b) The reason for not making any visit to the king can be understood that the king might have died by the time, i.e., AD 637-8 when Hiuen Tsang visited Magadha.

(c) In his Archaeological Survey Reports for 1871-2 and for 1879-80 General Cunningham places Pūrṇavarmā to the AD 590, and AD 630 differently.

(d) Therefore, Telang prefers AD 590, as the date of king

Pūrṇavarmā because if he was alive Hiuen Tsang might have visited him.

2. (a) Hiuen Tsang stated that king Śaśāṅka murdered Rājyavardhana, the elder brother of Harṣavardhana.

(b) Max-Müller has fixed the date of Rājyavardhana to the period between AD 600 and 610.

(c) King Śaśāṅka has destroyed the great *bodhi* tree at Bodha-Gayā. It was stated that it was reinvigorated during the time of king Pūrṇavarmā.

(d) Therefore, Pūrṇavarmā's period was earlier to Śaṅkara, who was a contemporary to Rājyavardhana.

(e) Hence, the period of Pūrṇavarmā was earlier to the destruction of the *bodhi* tree or definitely before the beginning of the seventh century AD.

3. (a) The Tamil Chronicle, *Kongudesarajakal* states that Śaṅkara converted king Tiruvikrama Deva I to Śaivism.

(b) Professor Dowson comments that it was not Tiruvikrama Deva I but Tiruvikrama Deva II who reigned in the eighth century AD (*JRAS*, vol. VIII, pp. 8, 16, 17) as mentioned in *The Indian Antiquary*, vol. XIII of April 1884 on page 99.

(c) On the basis of information derived from certain copper-plates, Professor Bhandarkar points out that king Tiruvikrama Deva I belongs to the fourth century and king Tiruvikramadeva II to the sixth century AD.

(d) The conclusion is that Śaṅkara must have flourished during the sixth century AD as he has converted king Tiruvikrama Deva II to Śaivism.

4. (a) Mādhavācārya, in his book *Śaṅkara Vijaya* (Canto VII, Stanza 60ff), mentions that Śaṅkara was an eyewitness of Kumārila Bhaṭṭa's self-immolation.

(b) According to the Tibetan sources, as stated by Dr. Burnell in his *Elements of South Indian Paleography*, Kumārila was a contemporary of Dharmakīrti, who flourished in the reign of Srong-tsan-gam-po, that extended from AD 629 to 658.

(c) Therefore, Śaṅkara and Kumārila might have lived in the latter half of the sixth century AD.

5. (a) Mādhavācārya's *Śaṅkara Vijaya* states that Śrī Harṣa, Bāṇa, Mayūra and Daṇḍī as the contemporaries of Śaṅkara.

(b) Professor Weber, Bühler and Max-Müller have placed Daṇḍī to the sixth century AD.

(c) Therefore, sixth century AD is the period in which Śaṅkara lived as a contemporary to Daṇḍī and others.

6. This argument is based upon the cultural history of China.

(a) Rev. S. Beal (in *JRAS* (N.S.). vol. XII, p. 355) states that during the Ch'en dynasty period, which continued from AD 557 to 583 in China, the Gauḍapāda *bhāṣya* on *Sāṁkhya-Kārikā* of Īśvara Kṛṣṇa was translated from Sanskrit to Chinese.

(b) H.T. Colebrooke mentions and it is also known from the Śaṅkara's commentary on *Māṇḍūkya-Kārikā* that Gauḍapāda was the teacher of Govinda, who in turn was a teacher to Śaṅkara.

(c) The translation has been made not during the lifetime of Gauḍapāda but probably after his death, i.e., during the time of his pupil Govinda. By this time Śaṅkara must have been listening to the lessons given by his teacher Govinda.

(d) This period of transition and the youthful years of Śaṅkara must be related to the Ch'en dynasty which ruled China from AD 557 to 583.

(e) Therefore, Śaṅkara must have lived during the latter half of the sixth century AD.

W. LOGAN'S ACCOUNT FROM KERALOTPATTI — DATE KNOWN TO ŚAṄKARA'S NATIVE LAND

On 4th February, 1887 W. Logan of Calicutt wrote to the editor of *The Indian Antiquary* informing that the 'Gracious Teacher' Śaṅkara's native land tradition is in accordance with the date fixed by K.B. Pathak. This was published in *The Indian Antiquary* in May 1887. Following are the reasons discussed by W. Logan:

1. The *Keralotpatti* recorded the history of Kerala. It says that Śaṅkarācārya, an incarnation of Lord Śiva, was born at the time of 'successful war'.

2. This 'successful war' was taken place during the reign of the king Perumal.

3. Again the *Keralotpatti* mentions that the same Cheraman Perumal embraced Islam and left for Mecca.

4. The *Tahafat-ul-Mujahidin*, an Arabian book that was written in latter half of the sixteenth century AD states that a king was buried at Zaphar.

5. People living at Zaphar say that a king namely Abdul Rahiman Samiri of Malabar was buried at Zaphar. And an inscription informs that in AH 212 he reached Zaphar and died there in 216.

6. As per Koran *Samiri* or Samaritan means worshipper of the calf. Probably the king, therefore, was no other but Cheraman Perumal.

7. The years of the AH 212 and 216 correspond with the years AD 827-8 and 831-2.

8. The Kollam Era of the Malayālī tradition began on 25th August AD 825. This probably relates to the great event of renouncing of the throne by king Cheraman.

9. It can be estimated that the period between his renouncing the throne in AD 825 and his arrival to Zaphar in AD 827 account for his travel.

10. Therefore, W. Logan concludes:

It follows from the above that if the 'gracious teacher' Śaṅkarācārya was, as Malayali tradition asserts, a contemporary of Cheraman Perumal, whose probable date was in the first quarter of the ninth century AD; and this agrees with Mr. K.B. Pathak's view of evidence cited by him.[5]

D.R. BHANDARKAR SUPPORTS K.B. PATHAK

After 20 years of K.B. Pathak's statement about the date of Śaṅkara, *The Indian Antiquary* of August 1912 has carried D.R. Bhandarkar's note in support of K.B. Pathak, Dr. D.R. Bhandarkar argues in the following way:[6]

Argument A

1. In the *Brahma-Sūtra-Bhāṣya* 4.3.5 and 2.4.1, Śaṅkara has mentioned the name Balavarman, who was probably his contemporary.
2. According to the Kodah copper-plate charter of Śaka 735, the Rāṣṭrakūṭa king, Govinda III gave a grant to a Jaina saint for his blessing against the aggression of neighbouring king Vimalāditya.
3. This Vimalāditya's grandfather was Balavarman.
4. If Vimalāditya belongs to Śaka 735, which corresponds AD 813, his grandfather Balavarman probably reigned 20 or 30 years earlier to him.
5. Then this 20 or 30 years earlier date corresponds to AD 793 or 783.
6. Therefore, Śaṅkarācārya probably belongs to this period.

---

5. W. Logan, 'The Dates of Śaṅkarācārya', an article in *The Indian Antiquary*, vol. XVI, May 1887, p. 161.
6. D.R. Bhandarkar, 'Can we fix the date of Śaṅkarācārya' in *The Indian Antiquary*, vol. XLI, August 1912, p. 200.

Argument B

1. Sarvajñātman has stated at the end of his work the *Śankṣepa-śārīraka* that it was written on the order of king Āditya.
2. It is probable that this Āditya is the same Vimalāditya mentioned in the Kodah copper-plate charter.
3. On the basis that Vimalāditya's grandfather was Balavarman and as well as 'Sarvajñātman's teacher's teacher was Śaṅkarācārya', it can be induced that king Balavarman and sage Śaṅkarācārya were contemporaries.
4. Hence, Śaṅkarācārya's period as stated here accord to the date proposed by K.B. Pathak.

Argument C

1. It is confirmed that Bhartṛhari, who was famous throughout India, died in AD 650.
2. Kumārila who criticised Bhartṛhari, actually belongs to half century later.
3. Similarly Śaṅkara who criticised Kumārila might have related to the next half century.
4. Hence, Śaṅkara might be one century junior to Bhartṛhari, probably related to AD 750.

NARASIMHACHAR EXCHANGE VIEWS WITH BHANDARKAR

Immediately after the publication of D.R. Bhandarkar's arguments about the date of Śaṅkara, R. Narasimhachar of Bangalore sent a note to the editor of the journal.[7]

In his note, R.N. Narasimhachar subscribes to the identification of Balavarman found in the *Brahma-Sūtra-Bhāṣya* of Śaṅkara with the Cālukya Chief, Balavarman who was referred to the Kadamba plates.

7. *The Indian Antiquary*, vol. XLII, February 1913, pp. 53-4.

However, Narasimhachar raises the point that Bālavarman was not only the king or name mentioned by Śaṅkara but several others like Jayasiṁha and Kṛṣṇa Gupta found place in the *Brahma-Sūtra-Bhāṣya* 4.3.5, 2.1.17.

On this point Bhandarkar says that there is no evidence to the effect that either the posterior or earlier kings do synchronise with either students or teachers of Śaṅkara.[8]

S.V. VENKATESWARAN ASSIGNS ŚAṄKARA TO NINTH CENTURY AD

In his letter dated 16th December 1913, S.V. Venkateswaran from Kumbakonam College wrote that the 'Āditya' word mentioned by Sarvajñātman was a part of compound noun in the names of Cālukya and Cola kings. Generally the word 'Āditya' referred to a powerful king; and among the two dynasties, the Cālukyas lost their fame earlier. Therefore, the powerful king referred to Āditya, might be a Cola king. Among the Colas, Parāntaka was the powerful king who reigned during the second half of the ninth century AD. If Sarvajñātman belongs to this period, his teacher's teacher, Śaṅkara might have related to the beginning of the ninth century AD. It is to be pointed out that Sarvajñātman administered the Kāñcī Monastery in the beginning; therefore, it is natural that Sarvajñātman might have got help from the Cola king.

Again during October 1914, S.V. Venkateswaran wrote that Śaṅkara might have lived during the ninth century AD for the following reasons:

1. The early Vaiṣṇava saints (Āḷvārs) like Śatagopa and Tirumaṅgai, who lived during eighth century AD, do not refer to Śaṅkara and his teachings. On the other hand, they criticised Śaiva, Sāṁkhya and Śākta schools.
2. The compiler of Vaiṣṇava songs, Nāthamuni and his followers criticised the doctrines of Śaṅkara.

---

8. *The Indian Antiquary*, vol. XLII, February 1913, p. 54.

3. It can be said that Śaṅkara must have lived before Nāthamuni and after the Vaiṣṇava saints (Āḷvars).
4. Nāthamuni is said to have been a contemporary of the Cola king Parantaka, who reigned, at the end of the ninth century AD.
5. Therefore, Śaṅkara might have lived in the first half of the ninth century AD.

Conclusion

The historical events confirm that Śaṅkarācārya was a contemporary to the king Cheraman Perumal of Kerala and Cola king Bālavarman, the grandfather of king Vimalāditya. And the literary evidences affirm that Śaṅkarācārya lived before Nāthamuni, the compiler of Vaiṣṇava songs. The arguments around these facts made by W. Logan, D.R. Bhandarkar, R. Narasimhachar and S.V. Venkateswaran assert the view that Śaṅkarācārya might have flourished between AD 750 and 850. When compared to the short span of Śaṅkarācārya's life and for the accuracy of facts, it is reasonable to consider the dates proposed by K.B. Pathak. Why because what K.B. Pathak discovered and what has been earlier stated by Prof. Teile and which was preserved in the Sanskrit *śloka*s through tradition (*sampradāya*) affirm that Śaṅkarācārya was born in AD 788 and died in AD 820.

Though K.T. Telang, with his much scholarship, rejects the above dates but agrees to the fact that they are based upon traditional verses recorded by eminent *paṇḍit*s. Traditional sources are many and differ about the date of Śaṅkarācārya but the traditional evidence provided by K.B. Pathak stands close to the historical facts. While K.B. Pathak's evidence speaks of definite point of time, K.T. Telang analyses the period of time. Eminent scholars of Indian Philosophy and History like S.N. Dasgupta, S.K. Belvalkar and K.A. Nilakantha Sastry have considered these dates because the traditional sources and the historical events synchronise.

4

The Times of Śaṅkarācārya

DUE to differences in fixing the date of Śaṅkarācārya, Duncan Greenness in his book, *The Gospel of Advaita* (1953) says, 'we do not know when Śaṅkarācārya lived'. However with due respect to the researches done by scholars and *paṇḍit*s, he concludes that the date of Śaṅkarācārya might be somewhere between AD 350 and 800. After a fresh examination of available evidences, Nakamura writes that AD 700-50 as the probable date of Śaṅkarācārya. Renou, Ingalls and some other distinguished scholars of Indology have accepted these dates.[1] Recently the editor of *Encyclopaedia of Indian Philosophies*, Karl H. Potter, especially on the basis of Allen Thrasher's study on Maṇḍana Miśra assigns Śaṅkarācārya to the late seventh or early eighth century AD.[2] Karl Potter argues that Śaṅkarācārya has referred to Kumārila, Bhartṛhari, Dharmakīrti and Gauḍapāda in his commentaries and it is accepted that they belonged to fifth, sixth and seventh centuries AD respectively. Therefore, Potter says that Śaṅkarācārya may be placed to the later period of seventh century AD or the beginning of the eighth century AD. This is in confirmation with the dates proposed by K.B. Pathak and many other scholars. During these times, with a consideration to AD 788 and AD 820 as the dates of Śaṅkarācārya, the social, political and religious conditions are worth studying.

---

1. Hajime Nakamura, *A History of Early Vedānta Philosophy*, 1983, Part One, p. 41.
2. Karl H. Potter, ed., *The Encyclopaedia of Indian Philosophies*, vol. III, 1981, p. 116.

Political and social conditions

Every thinker is a product of the social and political conditions of his times; and Śaṅkarācārya does not stand above the conditions of society. It is generally accepted fact that Śaṅkarācārya came from the village called Kālāḍī, on the banks of river Periyaru in the state of Kerala. During the fourth to eighth centuries AD in south India, the dominating powers were the Pallavas of Kāñcī and the Pāṇḍyas of Madurā. The Chera country was almost at many times under the suzerainty of the Pallavas and Pāṇḍyas. The history of Chera is obscure during these times and mutual conflict among the kingdoms was the dominant political fact.

With reference to the north India, during the period of Guptas, AD 319-447, the glory of India reached to its zenith. This period is considered as the golden age of India as there was revival of Vedic way of life, art and literature. Samudragupta (AD 330-80) was one of the most brilliant conquerors and ruled a larger part of India. He invaded the south and subdued many kings. After the Gupta period, Harṣa was the powerful king ruled from Kanauj during the first decade of seventh century AD. In this period there were powerful rulers in the south. When Harṣa invaded the south, the Cālukya king, Pulakeśin II defeated him. Subsequently, after some time Pallava ruler, Narasiṁhavarman I (AD 638-68) defeated Pulakeśin II and occupied his capital, Bādāmī. Later, one of the Pulakeśin's successors, Vikramāditya II carried a war and occupied the Pallava capital for some time in AD 740.[3] This reflected in the following verse of Śaṅkarācārya:

> There is at present no prince ruling over the whole earth.[4]

The social and political conditions of this period was generally

---

3. For this information, I rely much upon chapter 3 of K.A. Nilakanta Sastry and G. Srinivasachari, *Life and Culture of the Indian People*, 1974.

4. *Brahma-Sūtra-Bhāṣya*, 1.3.33. Cf., Swāmī Gambhīrānanda, tr., *Brahma-Sūtra-Bhāṣya of Śrī Śaṅkarācārya*, 1997, p. 228.

characterised by an extravagant and luxurious life of kings and courts and deprived the life of the majority of population. There is much inscriptional evidence for the superior position of brāhmaṇas and the respect shown to them and the gifts lavished on them by the princes and merchants. Pallava inscriptions mention the grants bestowed to Āpastambīa and Baudhaynīya brāhmaṇas. The Dharmaśāstras had acquired authority from the Pallava times in the south India. Higher learning of Sanskrit received patronage, whereas there was no evidence for encourage -ment for vocational training, etc., Kāñcīpuram became the centre for learning of Sanskrit. Temples were the popular places for worship and became centres of cultural activities. Exposition of Itihāsa-Purāṇas in the temples provided the people to acquaint themselves with the cultural values and tradition. Arts, crafts and commerce were organised on the basis of caste-guilds.[5]

Religious conditions

The medieval religious history of India reveals the theistic tendencies in Hinduism. As there was social, economic and cultural development in the Gupta period, religious revivalism took place. This was continued till the end of tenth century AD.

In south India different dynasties, ruling various states of the Deccan have patronised the Vaiṣṇava faith. The name of a Pallava king of Kāñcī is Viṣṇugopa, and the name Viṣṇukuṇḍina dynasty indicates the king's affiliation to that faith. The Bādāmī cave shrine contains various Vaiṣṇava images. The Vākāṭaka king, Rudrasena II became a devotee of Viṣṇu, though many Vākāṭaka kings were followers of Śiva. The Durgā temple at Aihole shows the development of Śaiva, Śākta and Vaiṣṇava cults. The Āḷvars, a body of Vaiṣṇava saints developed songs for the devotion of Lord Viṣṇu. These songs were composed in Tamil and attracted people. They advocated self-surrender to God through devotion (*bhakti*).

---

5. For further information see chapter VIII and XIII of K.A. Nilakanta Sastry, *A History of South India*, 1966 and chapter X of K.M. Panikkar, *A Survey of Indian History*, 1963.

The princes and people also patronised Śaivism throughout the country. According to an inscription on the base of a *śiva-liṅga* found near the village of Karamdaṇḍa in Faizābād district of Uttar Pradesh, the worship of Śiva was flourished during the time of Kumāragupta I. The Hūṇa chief Mihirakula was a devotee of Śiva. The devotees of Śiva in the south India are known as Nayanārs. The ardent devotees of Śiva developed Śaivism; they composed songs in the regional languages, especially in Tamil, and recruited people from all castes of the society. The Pallava kings too patronised the Śaiva cult.

There was also Śakti cult in certain parts of the country. The mother goddess (Durgā), killing the buffalo-demon was carved in a cave at Udayagiri, dated AD 401. An inscription of sixth century AD found at Deogarh in Jhānsī district of Madhya Pradesh contains a row of seven mothers. Early Kadambas and early Cālukyas were to some extent the followers of the Śāktism. Śakti cult was widespread throughout India. J.N. Banerjea remarks that Śakti cult was flourished in south India. Sculptures of different aspects of the Devī in the early temples of Bādāmī, Mahābalipuram, Ellorā and other places indirectly support the conclusion.[6] There was also another cult worshipping Gaṇeśa as the form of Śiva. Though it was not popular but flourished in some form or the other in the post-Gupta period.

Jainism enjoyed a good deal of royal patronage in the Deccan. Pulakeśin II of the Cālukya dynasty patronised the Jaina poets. Rāṣṭrakūṭas and Kadambas have paid grants to the Jaina temples. Eminent women from royal families followed Jainism. Not only in the state of Karnāṭaka but also in the extreme south India, Jainism was cherished. In the early centuries of the Christian era, Kāñcī was an important centre of Jaina culture. In AD 470 Draviḍasaṁgha was started at southern Madurā; and about one thousand years Jaina faith was deep routed in Tamil Nadu. However, later in the Pallava and Pāṇḍya kingdoms Jains have suffered and persecuted by Śaiva and Vaiṣṇava followers.

---

6. *Vide* his chapter 'Vaishnavism, Saivism and Minor Sects' in R.C. Mujumdar, *A Comprehensive History of India*, vol. III, part II, 1982, p. 809.

Buddhism flourished during the Kuṣāṇa period in the north and Sātavāhana period in south India. Dhanyakaṭaka region became the centre for Buddhism in Andhra Pradesh. Recent excavations in Viśākhāpatnam and West Godāvarī districts affirm the view that Buddhism spread in the coastal districts of Andhra Pradesh in ancient times. In the middle of seventh century AD, again after Kuṣāṇas and Gupta kings Buddhism flourished. Hiuen Tsang, a Buddhist pilgrim from China came to India and spent nearly fourteen years (AD 630-44) visiting many places starting from north India to the south. King Harṣavardhana who ascended the throne in AD 606 was a great patron of Buddhism. After third or fourth century AD, some Buddhists took to the study of systematic logic and began to criticise the doctrines of Vedic logicians. Diññāga, the Buddhist logician of AD 500, and the Sarvāstivadins and Sautrāntikas of Buddhism started to criticise the Vedic logicians. Thus, India witnessed the rise of many religious cults — both the *vaidika* and *avaidika*, before the advent of Śaṅkarācārya on the cultural map of India.

Mīmāṁsā School elaborated the Vedic rituals during the time of Śaṅkarācārya. Prabhākara and Kumārila, probably, may belong to the times of Śaṅkara. Prabhākara wrote commentary on the *Śābara-Bhāṣya* and Kumārila also wrote *Ślokavārttika*, *Tantravārttika* and *Tuptika* on the *Śābara-Bhāṣya*. The next leading exponent of Mīmāṁsā school, in the times of Śaṅkara, is Maṇḍana Miśra. He wrote *Vidhi-viveka*, *Mīmāṁsānukramaṇī* and *Tantravārttika*. The Mīmāṁsā School advocates Vedic rituals with methods of ascertaining validity and subscribing rules of interpretation. Hinduism was reorganised under the Brāhmaṇic priests by the doctrines expounded by these thinkers. Maṇḍana Miśra upheld the value of being a householder and practiser of all the duties prescribed by the Vedas. He criticised the doctrines of *jñāna-mārga* and *saṁnyāsa* and contested with Śaṅkarācārya in discussions.

Besides these Schools of religious thought, Śaṅkarācārya refer to the materialists known as Lokāyatas. In his introduction to the *Brahma-Sūtra-Bhāṣya* he states that the people were confused with different systems of religious thought, particularly the Lokāyatas who assert the body as the self or the self is a by-product of the body. There are no books available on the doctrines of Lokāyatas, but knowledge about them was found in the literature of other schools of religious thought. Lokāyata means 'common folk' and 'Lokāyata *mata*' referred to the 'view of common folk' by its opponents. In these circumstances, Śaṅkara attempted to expose the contradictions and tried to show the real message of ancient scriptures of India, i.e., the Upaniṣads.

Before and during the times of Śaṅkarācārya, there was gradual assimilation of Āryan institutions and ideas. The kingdoms of Deccan acted as bridge between the south and north, facilitating the transmission of ideas from one area to the other. According to the earlier inscriptions, a Pallava king performed Vedic sacrifice, *Aśvamedha* that proves the acceptance of certain aspects of Āryan culture. In the early part of this period AD 500-900, Jains and Buddhists controlled education, but gradually the brāhmaṇas superseded them. In addition, Mahendravarman I lost interest in Jainism and took up the cause of Śaivism. A seventh-century inscription of a Cālukya king at Bādāmī mentions Kannaḍa as the local native language and Sanskrit as the language of cultured. There was also religious movements propagated by groups of popular preachers, who are the Tamil saints called Āḷvars and Nayanārs. As a reaction to this, the *mīmāṁsaka*s came as keepers of Vedic tradition, and found their support by the kings of the south. The Tamil kings were convinced by the brāhmaṇas than the claims of the indigenous priests. Thus, the Vedic rituals reinforced. At this time Śaṅkarācārya came and sought to clean the Vedic philosophy of its obscurities and inconsistencies, and thereby, make it both comprehensive and acceptable to the people at large.

5

The Life of Śaṅkarācārya

A STUDY of the history of south India reveals that in the times of Śaṅkarācārya there was no powerful king in south India. This helped the people to move freely from one kingdom to another; and religious freedom was more in the case of priests and saints. This period noticed the rise of *bhakti* movement. Sanskrit learning continued in the religious centres like Kāñcīpuram. Brāhmaṇas were the dominating group of people through their behaviour and divinely oriented life. Kings and princes, merchants and the rich people have respected the brāhmaṇa priests. Temples have become the centres of Sanskrit learning apart from being the places of worship. The south Indian masses were attracted to brāhmaṇa rituals and behaviour, and Sanskritisation of the south was started. This has influenced the young Śaṅkarācārya; and a great thinker, theologian and philosopher has emerged. Accordingly Radhakrishnan states:

> Great thinkers appear in all great ages, and are as much the creatures as the creators of the era. Their genius lies in the power to seize the opportunity of the hour and give voice to the inarticulate yearnings that have been for long struggling in the hearts of men for expression. A creative thinker of the first rank, Śaṅkara entered into the philosophic inheritance of his age, and reinterpreted it with special reference to its needs.[1]

---

1. Radhakrishnan, *Indian Philosophy*, vol. II, 1966, p. 466.

Sources

There are a number of traditional biographies of Śaṅkarācārya as *Śaṅkara-Vijaya*s, and the prominent among them are *Śaṅkara-Dig-Vijaya* written by Mādhavācārya and *Śaṅkara-Vijaya* by Ānandagiri. Swāmī Tapasyānanda in his introduction to the translation of *Śaṅkara-Dig-Vijaya by Mādhavācārya* recorded ten prominent biographies of Śaṅkarācārya[2] and remarks that the one written by Mādhavācārya is a biographical and philosophical poem.[3] The author of the life of Śaṅkarācārya, Mādhavācārya whose text was placed in high esteem among the biographies was identified with Vidyāraṇya, who was the advisor to the founder of Vijayanagara empire and who became the head of the Śṛṅgerī monastery.

The *Śaṅkara-Dig-Vijaya* of Mādhava-Vidyāraṇya seems to be a modern text, narrating the life of Śaṅkarācārya systematically.The subject is treated in sixteen chapters, divided as follows:

First,	Prologue;
Second,	Birth of Śaṅkarācārya;
Third,	Earthly manifestation of the Devas;
Fourth,	Life story up to the age of eight;
Fifth,	Adopting *saṁnyāsa*;
Sixth,	Establishment of the pristine philosophy of Self-knowledge;
Seventh,	Meeting Vyāsa;
Eighth,	Controversy with Maṇḍana;
Ninth,	Establishing claims to universal knowledge in the presence of Sarasvatī;
Tenth,	Acquirement of knowledge of sex-love;
Eleventh,	Encounter with the Fierce Bhairava;
Twelfth,	The coming of some disciples;
Thirteenth,	Preaching of *Brahma-vidyā*;

2. Śrī Swāmī Tapasyānanda, tr., *Śaṅkara-Dig-Vijaya by Mādhava-Vidyāraṇya*, Fifth impression, p. viii.
3. *Ibid.*, p. ix.

Fourteenth, Pilgrimages of Padmapāda;
Fifteenth, Triumphal Tour; and
Sixteenth, Accession to Śāradāpīṭha.[4]

Life at glance

Śaṅkarācārya was born in a family of Nambūdiri brāhmaṇa sect in a village called Kālāḍī in the State of Kerala. His parents Śivaguru and Āryāṁba were pious couple having deep religious culture that was usual among the Nambūdrī brāhmaṇas. In those times among the Nambūdrī families every boy received necessary training in Vedic recital and study. Śaṅkara was born after his parents made a pilgrimage to Śiva-Kṣetra, Trichur; hence named after the Lord Śiva. Mādhavācārya recorded it that one day Lord Śiva appeared to Śivaguru in a dream. Being satisfied with the prayers, Śiva awarded a boon to choose 'either an all-knowing and virtuous but short lived son or one who would live very long but without any special virtue or greatness'.[5] Śivaguru chose the earlier and endowed with Śaṅkara. Further the *Śaṅkara-Dig-Vijaya* records that Śaṅkara attained proficiency in languages in his first year, and mastered the *kāvya*s and Purāṇas by the second year. He was given *upanayanam* at the age of five and subsequently he learnt the four Vedas and the six Śāstras. Mādhavācārya records:

> In the knowledge of Vedas he was like a Brahma; of its auxiliaries, like Gārgya; of sacred narratives, like Bṛhaspati; of the doctrines on rituals, like Jaimini; and of philosophy, like Bādarāyaṇa.[6]

A number of miracles are associated with the life of Śaṅkara. One day a group of sages came to his house and explained to his mother that he would not live long. According to the divine wish Śaṅkara had to become a mendicant, *saṁnyāsin*; but his mother was not interested in his becoming a *saṁnyāsin*. Śaṅkara wanted

---

4. *Śaṅkara-Dig-Vijaya*, Canto-1, 18-26, *ibid.*, pp. 3-4.
5. *Ibid.*, Canto-2, 46-53, *ibid.*, p. 14.
6. *Ibid.*, Canto-4, 1, *ibid.*, p. 28.

to become a *saṁnyāsin*. One day a miracle happened: When Śaṅkara was taking bath in a nearby river, a crocodile caught hold of his leg and dragged him; his mother saw and cried. Then Śaṅkara asked his mother to give permission to take *saṁnyāsa*, so that the crocodile might leave him as he was going to become a *saṁnyāsin* according to the divine wish. At this crucial hour his mother Āryāṁba agreed, and he was released from the jaws of the crocodile dramatically. Thus Śaṅkara had become a *saṁnyāsin* to take up his chosen divine mission.

Subsequently Śaṅkara travelled the whole of India. He met Govinda at the banks of river Narmadā and stayed with him for sometime as a disciple. At this place Śaṅkara had the opportunity of listening to Gauḍapāda who wrote verse commentary (*kārikā*) on the *Māṇḍūkya Upaniṣad*. Next Saṅkara proceeded to north India and visited a number of holy places. His biographers write that Śaṅkara wrote commentaries on the Upaniṣads, the *Bhagavad Gītā* and the *Brahma Sūtra* in Benāras. There he reached the heights of a teacher and had Padmapāda, Sureśvara and Hastāmalaka as his disciples.

Encounter with an outcast

At this juncture Mādhavācārya's *Śaṅkara-Dig-Vijaya* records Śaṅkara's encounter with an outcast as follows:

> On one noon, the great ācārya, walked with his disciples to the Gaṅgā. . . . On their way, the party came across a hunter, an outcast, approaching them with his pack of four dogs. They ordered him to move away. But the hunter raised an issue. He asked: "You are always going about preaching that the Vedas teach the non-dual *Brahman* to be the only reality. If this is so, how has this sense of difference overtaken you? There are hundreds of *saṁnyāsin*s going about, indulging in high sounding philosophical talk. But not even a ray of knowledge having found entrance into their hearts, their holy exterior serves only a dupe householders. You asked me to move aside and make a way for you. To whom

> were your words addressed O learned Sir? to the body that comes from the same source and performs the same functions in the case of both a Brāhmaṇa and an outcast? Or to the *Ātma*, the witnessing consciousness, which too is the same in all unaffected by anything that is of the body? How does such differences as 'This is a Brāhmaṇa, this is an outcast' arise in non-dual experience. O revered teacher! Is the sun changed in the least, if it reflects in a liquor pot or in the holy Gaṅgā? How can you indulge in such false sentiments as, 'Being a Brāhmaṇa I am pure; and you, dog-eater, must therefore, give way for me' when the truth is that the one universal and unblemishable spirit, himself bodiless, is shining alike in all bodies." . . .[7]

When the outcast finished his argument, Śaṅkarācārya spoke as follows:

> All that you have said is true. You are, indeed, one of the noblest of men. Your words of wisdom make me abandon the idea that you are an outcast. . . . A person who sees the whole world as *ātma* only, whose mind is (un-shake-able) established in that conviction is worthy of worship, irrespective of whether he is a Brahmana or an outcast by birth.[8]

While Śaṅkarācārya was writing commentary on the *Brahma Sūtra*, Vyāsa appeared as an old man and asked him to defend and preach the Advaita Vedānta to refute all hostile doctrines. A reference is as follows:

> There are many more learned men, leaders of hostile schools of thought, whom you have not yet defeated in debate. Your life has to be prolonged for some years, so that you may triumph over them also.[9]

---

7. *Śaṅkara-Dig-Vijaya*, Canto-6, 20-32, *ibid.*, pp. 59-60.
8. *Ibid.*, 33-9, *ibid.*, p. 60.
9. *Ibid.*, Canto-7, 51-8, *ibid.*, p. 74.

Religious harmony and travels

The religious theology of Śaṅkarācārya can be seen from his practical side of life. Not only the background but the life of Śaṅkara, particularly his missionary activities shows that he was a committed man for a unified religion with the united theological ways. He wrote not only commentaries on the *prasthānatrayī*, but also selected prominent part of each type of literature the Śruti, Smṛti and Sūtras. This outlook of Śaṅkara made him to visit various temples and places to establish a unified theology in India. Commenting on the biography of Śaṅkara, Duncan Greenless[10] and T.M.P. Mahadevan[11] mentioned that his travels throughout India resulted in promoting religious harmony among the Hindus. This is evident from his tours of victory. He met the followers of Śaiva sects in Rāmeśvaram; he encountered with the Kāpālikas at Ujjain; discussed with the believers of Gaṇapati in Puraṅgavaram; argued with people in the temple of Mallikārjuna in Śrīśailam. The essence of his arguments is that *Brahman* is one and people are worshipping in different names. This is aptly put forward by T.M.P. Mahadevan:

> Like philosophy, religion too profited by Śaṅkara's teachings. While he sought to remove the excessiveness that had crept into the faiths and their institutions he desired to conserve them in their purity as but various modes of approach to God. The conception of a personal Deity is not the highest, according to Śaṅkara. But God, for him, is neither an irrelevance nor a concession to the mob.[12]

Śaṅkarācārya was not to be a critic by denying the personal God and worship, but interested to establish unity among the systems. His mission is not to bring quarrel among various theological systems but to see that a spirit of unity prevails. He interpreted

---

10. Duncan Greenless, *The Gospel of Advaita*, 1953, pp. xxxvi-xxxix.
11. T.M.P. Mahadevan, *Śaṅkarācārya*, 1968, *vide*: chapters III and IV.
12. *Ibid*., p. 31.

the theology of the Upaniṣads and preached it for the benefit of humanity, as people are misguided with false doctrines.

Śaṅkarācārya, it is said that, has popularised the *pañcāyatana* form of worship. This form of worship relates to select one deity among five and the main worship is concentrated upon the *iṣṭa devatā* or 'chosen deity' while the other four are together worshipped. Śaṅkarācārya said to his disciples to practice the same. He visited a number of holy places in north and south India connected to the Vaiṣṇava, Śaiva and Śākta sects. He visited the temple of Mysore State and discussed with the priests and analysed to them that there was no difference between Viṣṇu and Śiva.[13] In his pilgrimage, Śaṅkarācārya installed Śrī Cakra in several temples, particularly in the Devī temple at Allāhābād, and Tripurasundarī temple at Tiruvayyur near Madras and Devī Kāmākṣī temple at Kāñcī. All these religious and devotional activities of Śaṅkarācārya prove that he was a devotee apart from being the believer of Advaita of Vedānta. He believes that worship of any deity is nothing but worshipping *Īśvara;* and *Īśvara*, Viṣṇu and Śiva are the triple aspects of the Absolute *Brahman*. The worship of the devotee to any one of these deities or gods is nothing but the worship of the lower nature of *Brahman*. This devotion and worship leads one to the highest goal, *mokṣa*. He advised the people to forget about the sectarian differences being decorating themselves with symbols and ashes but turn to the higher level of worship.

Hinduism is a religion of many cults and different deities. At different places in India, various gods are worshipped according to the nature of the people. The form of worship also differs from one place to the other place. There are contradictions apparently but there is a fundamental belief that the God, they worship, is an incarnation, *avatāra* of the Supreme Being, *Brahman*. The claim of Śaṅkarācārya is that though Hinduism consists of several cults there should not be any conflict among them. He established a harmonious relation among various cults

---

13. *Śaṅkarācārya*, p. 46.

and therefore, he was called the establisher of the six faiths, *ṣaṇmata-sthāpak-ācārya*.[14]

Śaṅkarācārya, in order to preach the message of Advaita Vedānta, had established missionary centres (monasteries) in the four corners of India, Badarīnāth in Himālayas, Dvārakā in Gujarat, Purī in Orissa and Śṛṅgerī in Mysore.

---

14. *Śaṅkarācārya*, p. 44.

6

The Works of Śaṅkarācārya

THERE has been a considerable debate regarding the authentic works of Śaṅkarācārya. Over five decades ago, Belvalkar declared that the commentaries of Śaṅkara on the following Upaniṣads — *Īśa*, *Kena*, *Kaṭha*, *Praśna*, *Muṇḍaka*, *Māṇḍūkya*, *Aitareya*, *Taittirīya, Chāndogya* and *Bṛhadāraṇyaka* have been genuine. According to him the *Brahma-Sūtra-Bhāṣya* is certainly the work of Śaṅkara and the commentary on the *Bhagavad Gītā* might be his own probably. Similarly Belvalkar believes that a few *prakaraṇa grantha*s are having a satisfactory claim to Śaṅkarācārya's authorship.[1]

Karl H. Potter, after examining the studies done by Paul Hacker and Sangeku Mayeda with reference to the words, context and conceptions of the works, concludes that the commentaries of Śaṅkara on the *Brahma Sūtra*, the *Bṛhadāraṇyaka* and the *Taittirīya Upaniṣad* as well as the *Upadeśa-sahasrī* are undoubtedly Śaṅkara's works. The commentaries on the *Aitareya,* the *Chāndogya,* the *Muṇḍaka* and the *Praśna Upaniṣad*s are also written by him.[2]

Paul Hacker and others questioned the authorship of Śaṅkara on the commentary of the *Bhagavad Gītā*. Ingalls and Raghavan believed that Śaṅkara wrote the commentary on the *Bhagavad*

---

1. S.K. Belvalkar, *Vedānta Philosophy*, Part I, 1929, pp. 217-30.
2. Karl H. Potter, *The Encyclopaedia of Indian Philosophies*, vol. III, 1981, p. 116.

Gītā, and Mayeda says that there was no sufficient reason to reject the authorship of Śaṅkarācārya.[3]

Paul Hacker's studies

Paul Hacker has studied the following series of publications and manuscripts on the question of Śaṅkara's authorship of certain works.[4]

1. A catalogue of the Sanskrit manuscripts in the Library of His Highness the Mahārājā of Bikaner, published in Calcutta 1880, edited by Rejendralal Mitra.
2. A descriptive catalogue of Sanskrit manuscripts in the Calcutta College (Vedic manuscripts 1895, Philosophy Manuscripts 1900 volumes) edited by Hrishikesa Sastri and Siva Chandra Gui.
3. A descriptive catalogue of the Sanskrit manuscripts in the Tanjore Maharaja Serfoji's Saraswati-Mahal Library, Tanjore, voll.I-XIX published at Srirangam 1928-34, edited by P.P.S. Sastri.
4. Reports on Sanskrit manuscripts in southern India, Nos. I-III, Madras 1895-1905 by E. Hultzsch.
5. Catalogue of the printed books and manuscripts in Sanskrit belonging to the oriental library of the Asiatic Society of Bengal, Calcutta published at Calcutta in 1904, edited by Kunjavihari Kavyatirtha.

Apart from these catalogues and reports, Paul Hacker has also consulted and considered the books connected with studies in Śaṅkara, published under the following series.

1. Anandasrama Sanskrit Series.
2. Bibliotheca Sanskrit Series.
3. Kasi Sanskrit Series.

---

3. *The Encyclopaedia of Indian Philosophies*, vol. III, p. 294.
4. Paul Hecker, 'Śaṅkarācārya and Śaṅkara-bhagavatpāda (preliminary remarks concerning the authorship problem)', in *The New Indian Antiquary*, pp. 175-86.

4. Vizianagaram Sanskrit Series.
5. Bombay Sanskrit Series.
6. Works of Sankaracharya, Poona Edition.
7. Nirnayasagar Press Series.

What is his name? and which is the title?

Many Vedāntic writers call the exponent of Advaita Vedānta as Śaṅkarācārya. But Paul Hacker has traced the evolution of the name Śaṅkarācārya. He writes that in ancient times Śaṅkarācārya was neither called by this name nor with a title *ācārya*.

At first his disciple Padmapāda in the introduction of his book, the *Pañcapādikā* mentioned his teacher as 'Śaṅkara', and another disciple Sureśvara also calls him 'Śaṅkara' in his *Naiṣkarmyasiddhi* (4.74,76). These two disciples used the titles — *bhāṣyakāra*, *bhāgavat*, *bhagavatpāda*, *bhagavat-pūjyapāda*. A contemporary of Śaṅkara, Vācaspatimiśra in his *Bhāmatī* states him *bhagavān bhāṣyakāra*. Jñānottama, a commentator on Sureśvara's *Naiṣkarmyasiddhi* mentions him, *bhāṣyakāra*, *bhagavatpādācārya*, *bhagavat-pūjyapāda-ācārya* and *ācārya* (Jñānottama's Commentary on *Naiṣkarmyasiddhi* 1.6; 4.20, 22, 23, 44). Satcidānanda Yogīndra, a commentator on the *Śruti-Sāra-samuddharaṇa* of Ṭoṭakācārya, a disciple of Śaṅkara states that the teacher of Ṭoṭakācārya was *bhagavatpāda*. Thus, the name 'Śaṅkarācārya' does not appear in the earlier commentaries and his disciples called him either by name Śaṅkara or by the title *bhagavat* or *bhāṣyakāra*. Even this tradition has been continued in the later Advaita literature also.

Paul Hacker has also noticed the specific character of Indian traditional writing. The Indian ancient writers, at the beginning or particularly at the end of a book or chapter use to state their names saying in colophons like 'This book has been written by so and so, the son of so and so, the disciple of so and so, by the order of so and so' and so on. Hence, in many cases it is easy to recognise the author of a text. With reference to Śaṅkara, owing to the different usage of names or the various titles, and due to the short period of his lifetime, the books that are attributed to him have been doubtful of his authorship.

Irrespective of the authorship problem, Paul Hacker considers Śaṅkara as the 'Great *bhāṣyakāra*' of Advaita Vedānta and propagator of the *māyā* doctrine. He says that except the *Brahma-Sūtra-Bhāṣya*, all other works attributed to him should be investigated as Śaṅkarācārya lived only for 32 years. Paul Hacker comments that many books were attributed to him due to the fact that every head of the Śṛṅgerī Monastery from time to time has been given the title 'Śaṅkarācārya'. There is also a point that some less renowned heads of the Monastery probably wished that their followers to call them by the sacred title 'Śaṅkarācārya'. Thus it is probable that many texts written by different heads or some others in later times might have been considered as written by Śaṅkarācārya, which lead in due course to attribute every text to the founder Śaṅkara.

Hacker concludes that the colophons of texts those describe the *bhagavat* as its composer are the genuine works of Śaṅkarācārya, in view of Śaṅkara's disciples or his contemporaries called him *bhagavat*, *bhagavat-pāda* and *bhagavat-pujyapāda*. The colophons of the *Brahma-Sūtra-Bhāṣya* have ascribed the same words. Hacker writes that the commentaries on the triple texts (*prasthānatrayī*) were also the genuine of his authorship. On the other hand, the texts attributed to 'Śaṅkarācārya' in their colophons were doubtful regarding their authorship of Śaṅkara. Apart from examining the colophons, Paul Hacker further states that the content, doctrines and phraseology of the texts are to be compared with that of the *Bhrama-sūtra-Bhāṣya* in order to establish their authorship of Śaṅkara.

Karma (action/ritual) has been given a prominent place in the commentary on the *Bhagavad Gītā* either as a subsidiary means to attain *mokṣa* or as a preliminary step to attain *mokṣa* through knowledge.[5] Similar to the thesis in the *Brahma-Sūtra-*

5. For further understanding refer to P. George Victor, *Social Philosophy of Vedānta*, 1991, p. 135.

Bhāṣya that knowledge alone leads to liberation, the *Bhagavad Gītā Bhāṣya* also emphasises knowledge but extensively discusses about *karma* (action).[6] Due to these facts, as noted by Karl H. Potter, the authorship of Śaṅkara on the *Bhagavad Gītā Bhāṣya* has been questioned. However, many researchers and Karl H. Potter agree that Śaṅkara wrote the *Bhagavad Gītā Bhāṣya*.[7]

The third volume of the *Encyclopaedia of Indian Philosophies* edited by Karl H. Potter devoted to Advaita Vedānta, maintains that the following texts without question be accepted as the texts of Śaṅkarācārya.[8]

The Brahma-Sūtra-Bhāṣya
The Bṛhadāraṇyaka Upaniṣad Bhāṣya
The Taittirīya Upaniṣad Bhāṣya
The Aitareya Upaniṣad Bhāṣya
The Chāndogya Upaniṣad Bhāṣya
The Muṇḍaka Upaniṣad Bhāṣya
The Praśna Upaniṣad Bhāṣya
The Upadeśa-sahasrī

The works apart from these are related to speculation, but Karl Potter includes in the volume the minor texts of Śaṅkarācārya, which is evident from the table of contents in his Encyclopaedia.[9] The famous texts *Vivekacūḍāmaṇi*, the *Sarva-Vedānta Siddhānta-sāra-saṁgraha* and the *Ātmabodha* have been considered for summation. Thus works attributed to Śaṅkarācārya are many and Karl H. Potter has enlisted them in the first volume of his *Encyclopaedia of Indian Philosophies.*[10]

Works attributed to Śaṅkarācārya

1. *Advaitānubhūti* (Advaita).
2. *Pañca-ratna* or *Ātma-pañcaka* or *Sopāna-pañcaka*.

---

6. *Social Philosophy of Vedānta*, p. 134.
7. Karl H. Potter, *op. cit.*, vol. III, p. 294.
8. *Ibid.*, p. 116.
9. *Ibid.*, pp. vii-viii.
10. Karl H. Potter, *op. cit.*, vol. I, pp. 82-111.

3. *Aitareya Upaniṣad Bhāṣya.*
4. *Ajñāna-bodhini* (Advaita).
5. *Anātma-śrīvigarhana-prakaraṇa.*
6. *Aparokṣānubhūti* (Advaita).
7. *Atharvaśikhā Upaniṣad Bhāṣya.*
8. *Atharvaśiro Upaniṣad Bhāṣya.*
9. *Ātma-bodha* (Advaita).
10. *Ātma-jñānopadeśa* (or *Triputi*) (Advaita).
11. *Ātmānātma-viveka* (Advaita).
12. *Bāla-bodha* (*Saṁgraha*) or *Bāla-bodhinī* (Advaita).
13. *Bhagavad Gītā Bhāṣya.*
14. *Brahma-Jñāna-valimala.*
15. *Brahmāṇu-cintana.*
16. *Brahma-Sūtra-Bhāṣya* (Advaita).
17. *Bṛhadāraṇyaka Upaniṣad Bhāṣya.*
18. *Chāndogya Upaniṣad Bhāṣya.*
19. *Dakṣiṇā-mūrti-stotra.*
20. *Daśa-ślokī* or *Nirvāṇa-daśaka.*
21. *Dhanyāṣṭaka.*
22. *Śaṅkarācārya-dvādaśa-ratna.*
23. *Eka-ślokī.*
24. *Bhāṣya on* Gauḍapāda's *Māṇḍūkya Kārika.*
25. *Guru-vaṣṭaka.*
26. *Hastāmalakiya Bhāṣya.*
27. *Īśa (vyāsa) Upaniṣad Bhāṣya.*
28. *Kaṭha Upaniṣad Bhāṣya.*
29. *Kaupīna-pañcaka* or *Yati-pañcaka.*
30. *Kena Upaniṣad Bhāṣya.*
31. *Manisa-pañcaka.*
32. *Māyā-pañcaka.*
33. *Māyā-vivaraṇa.*
34. *Muṇḍaka Upaniṣad Bhāṣya.*
35. *Nirvāṇa Mañjarī.*

36. *Nirvāṇāṣṭaka* or *Ātmaśataka*.
37. *Nṛsiṁhottaratāpanī Bhāṣya*.
38. *Pañcīkaraṇa* (Advaita).
39. *Paramārtha-sāra*.
40. *Praśna Upaniṣad Bhāṣya*.
41. *Prauḍhānubhūti*.
42. *Sadācāra-aṇu-saṁdhāna*.
43. *Śata-ślokī*.
44. *Svarūpa-aṇu-saṁdhāna*.
45. *Svātama-nirūpaṇa*.
46. *Svātma-prakāśikā*.
47. *Śvetāśvatara Upaniṣad Bhāṣya*.
48. *Taittirīya Upaniṣad Bhāṣya*.
49. *Tattva-bodha* or *Tattva-upadeśa*.
50. *Upadeśa-sahasrī* (Advaita).
51. *Vajra-sūcyopaniṣad Bhāṣya*.
52. *Vākya-sudhā* or *Dṛg-dṛśya-viveka* (Advaita).
53. *Vākya-vṛtti* (Advaita).
54. *Viveka-cūḍāmaṇi* (Advaita).
55. *Yoga-tārāvalī*.

7

Śaṅkarācārya on the Upaniṣads

Yājñavalkya and Maitreyī Dialogue

THE dialogue between Yājñavalkya and Maitreyī regarding the Pantheistic-Self appears in two different chapters of the *Bṛhadāraṇyaka Upaniṣad.* Yājñavalkya was a theologian and *paṇḍit* in the court of king Janaka. He has two wives — Maitreyī and Kātyāyanī. He discusses about the Pantheistic-Self, *Brahman* as the inner controller of the universe and many related issues in the court with the king and other *paṇḍit*s.

TEXT SUMMARY[1]

In this dialogue with his wife — Maitreyī, Yājñavalkya expresses his desire to renounce the householder state (*gṛhastha āśrama*) and wishes to be a forest dweller (*vānaprastha āśrama*). Hence Yājñavalkya wants to divide his property among his two wives and invites his wife Maitreyī and said so. Maitreyī being a discussant on *Brahman* (*Brahma-vādinī*) questions Yājñavalkya weather wealth would help her to attain immortality? Yājñavalkya replies that immortality cannot be attained through the wealth; on the other hand, he asserts that wealth helps one to lead a comfortable life, and nothing more. Then Maitreyī questions him about the validity of wealth to her by loosing her dear husband.

In his analytical answer, Yājñavalkya says to his wife

1. The Textual Summary is based upon R.E. Hume, *The Thirteen Principal Upaniṣads*, 1949.

Maitreyī that husband and wife are dear (*priya*) to each other due to the love of one's own self (*ātma*), but not due to love on each other. In the same way he says that sons, wealth and cattle are dear (*priya*) due to one's love for the self. The status of being a brāhmaṇa or kṣatriya and the status being associated with the world, gods, Vedas and beings — is dear to us because of our love of the self (*ātma*). (In ordinary experience on the basis of empirical relation and for physical purpose, we can also interpret that members in a family or in the society are dear to each other because they are benefited being close and dear. In other words, husband and wife are dear to each other because of their self-benefits. For the sake of self-fulfilment one loves the other; hence arose co-operation and dearness).

Yājñavalkya says that one has to know the self, especially one should see, hear, think and ponder over the self (*ātma*).[2] This is *śravaṇa* (listening), *manana* (repetition) and *nididhyāsana* (meditation) as often quoted by Śaṅkarācārya and other vedāntins.

If the self is known, everything in the world is known. Similarly if the self is unknown everything in the world is unknown. In a sound produced through either a drum, or a conch-shell or a *vīṇā*, there will be a number of sound waves and distinct notes or various tones in the general sound produced. From a fire of wet woods different smokes arose. Likewise, Yājñavalkya says that from the great Being (*ātma*) the four Vedas, Upaniṣads, Itihāsa-Purāṇas, Sūtras, and Vyākhyānas were born. The great Being is the source of all things in the world. The great Being is like the sea into which different waters of various rivers flow. Similarly, it is like skin for different touchness, tongue for all tastes, mind for all intentions, heart for all knowledge, hands for all actions, feet for all journeys, speech for all Vedas, generative organ for all pleasures, eye for all perception, nose for all smells and ear for all sounds. The great Being is a mass of knowledge (*vijñāna-ghana*) like water that is salty, after a lump of salt dissolved in it.

---

2. *Bṛhadāraṇyaka Upaniṣad*, 2.4.5. & 4.5.6. (All the references are cited from R.E. Hume, *op.cit.*, pp. 100-45).

In conclusion, Yājñavalkya says that things cannot be understood if perceived differently/dual. If there is difference between what exists actually and the perception based upon it, it is a duality (*dvaita*). If there is duality one sees a thing as other thing. Similarly, dual-cognition in thinking, understanding and speaking leads to difference against the actuality. Yājñavalkya says, if everything in the world becomes just as one's own self, then it is not possible to see, hear, think and understand differently. Then there will be no perceiver and perceived, subject and object, the wise man and the knowledge. This is the message spoken by Yājñavalkya to Maitreyī for attaining immortality. Yājñavalkya further proclaims that *Brahman* is beyond human cognition and definition. He says:

> That soul (*ātmā*) is not this, it is not that (*neti, neti*). It is unseizable, for it cannot be seized; indestructible, for it cannot be destroyed; unattached, for it does not attach itself; is unbound, does not tremble, is not injured.[3]

ŚAṄKARĀCĀRYA'S COMMENTARY[4]

Śaṅkarācārya says that this debate of Yājñavalkya and Maitreyī is introduced to assert that renunciation of everything is a part of the knowledge of the self to attain immortality.[5] It is also established that immortality is independent of rites/actions/rituals.

Śaṅkarācārya points out that the Vedas speak of both the performance of rites and renunciation of rites. But the knowledge of the self alone leads to immortality; therefore one should not perform rites. In fact, Yājñavalkya was a follower of rituals in the beginning, later he desired to renounce the world. Vyāsa in the *Mahābhārata* said: 'Men are bound by rites and freed by knowledge. Hence sages who have known the truth never

---

3. *Bṛhadāraṇyaka Upaniṣad*, 2.4.5; 4.5.6.
4. Summarised from Swāmī Mādhavānanda, tr., *The Bṛhadāraṇyaka Upaniṣad with the commentary of Śaṅkarācārya*, 1965, pp. 348-76 and 771-96.
5. *Ibid.*, p. 349.

perform rites'.[6] This follows that renunciation of this world is enjoined as a subsidiary step. The self (*ātman*) is the domain of the knowledge of *Brahman*, and unattached by all differences and material qualities. Being *Brahman* thus, it can be explained as 'not this, not this'. Yājñavalkya condemns wealth and rites, and expresses that one should cultivate distaste for wife, husband and sons, etc.

In this context, Śaṅkarācārya says that the self is worthy of realisation, as propounded by Yājñavalkya and also in the sentence: 'I am *Brahman*'. He writes:

> It should first be heard of from a teacher and from the scriptures, then reflected upon through reasoning, and then meditated upon.[7]

According to Śaṅkarācārya, the relative existence of the self or the particular consciousness of the self is due to ignorance. This is due to the superimposition of the limiting adjuncts — the body and organs, etc., upon the self. In this state of ignorance man attaches himself to castes and orders of life related to ends and means, name and form. In this context Śaṅkara says:

> The different castes such as the brāhmaṇa or the kṣatriya, the various orders of life, and so on, upon which rites depend, and which consists of actions, and their factors and results, are objects of notions superimposed on the self by ignorance, i.e., based on false notions like that of a snake in a rope.[8]

Śaṅkarācārya says that in reality the individual self is nothing but the Supreme Self, *Brahman*. *Brahman* is there before the

---

6. *The Bṛhadāraṇyaka Upaniṣad with the commentary of Śaṅkarācārya*, p. 350. (Cf., *Mahābhārata*, XII, CCXLVII. 1-2).
7. *Bṛhadāraṇyaka Upaniṣad Bhāṣya*, 2.4.5. All the references related to this commentary are from Swāmī Madhavānanda, tr., *The Bṛhadāraṇyaka Upaniṣad, with the commentary of Śaṅkarācārya*, 1965.
8. *Ibid.*, 2.4.5.

origin of the world, it is nothing but *Brahman*. The world is emanated from *Brahman* like the sparks, smoke and flames from fire, similar to the waters of rivers, tanks and lakes that flow and dissolved in ocean, loosing their particular entity. The separate existence of the self or the individualised entity will be destroyed when the realisation of *Brahman* attained. Thus the particular consciousness does not exist. Śaṅkara remarks that in the presence of particular or individual aspect of the self there is duality (*dvaita*). After the realisation of the unity of the self and the Supreme Self, *Brahman* there cannot be any consciousness of actions and separate-assumed-existence of the individual.

Yājñavalkya and Gārgī dialogue[9]

Yājñavalkya was a great theologian (*brahma-vettha*) in the court of king Janaka of Videha. Discussions on theology (*brahma-vidyā*) were held in the courts and assemblies of kings and princes. The dialogue between Yājñavalkya and Vācaknavī, the daughter of Gārgī is one of the series of discussions undertaken by Yājñavalkya in the court of king Janaka, recorded in the third chapter of the *Bṛhadāraṇayaka Upaniṣad.*

TEXT SUMMARY

King Janaka performed a great sacrifice (*yajña*) for which theologians (*brahma-vettha*s) of Kuru and Pañcāla kingdoms have attended. The king wanted to award one thousand cows, having gold coverings to their horns for the winner among theologians. Being confident, Yājñavalkya orders his disciple, Samaśravas to drive away the cows. The rest of the theologians felt angry and bitterly questioned him. Yājñavalkya stood firm to their encounter and answers appropriately and proved himself 'the most learned in scriptures'.

9. *Bṛhadāraṇyaka Upaniṣad*, 3.6; 3.8. All the references related to this text are from R. E. Hume, *The Thirteen Principal Upaniṣads*, 1949.

Yājñavalkya answers the questions:

(1) To the first question of Aśvala, the *hotṛ* priest, relating to the rules pertaining to performance of sacrifice, Yājñavalkya replies with all details relating to sacrifice.

(2) Yājñavalkya declares, to Jartakarva Artabhāga's question, that when man dies only the name remains.

(3) To the third question by Bhujyu Lahayayāni relating to the destination of the offerings in horse-sacrifice, Yājñavalkya answers that the Indra world is the destination of the offerings made in horse-sacrifice.

(4) To the question of Uṣasta Cakrayāna, Yājñavalkya asserts that *Brahman* cannot be known, on the other hand It is immanent in all things, including the body of Uṣasta Cakrayāna.

(5) To the fifth question of Kahola Kauṣitakeya about the practical way of knowing *Brahman*, for which Yājñavalkya asserts renunciation as means to the knowledge of *Brahman*.

(6) Gārgī Vācaknavi, as the sixth contender, questions about the ultimate source and base of the world; for which Yājñavalkya asserts *Brahman* as the ultimate source and base of the world.

(7) Uddālaka Āruṇi questions about the inner controller of the world, for which Yājñavalkya replies as follows:

He is the unseen Seer, the unheard Hearer, the unthought Thinker, the un-understood Understander. Other than He there is no Seer. Other than He there is no Hearer. Other than He there is no Thinker. Other than He there is no Understander. He is your Soul, the Inner Controller, the Immortal.[10]

10. *Bṛhadāraṇyaka Upaniṣad*, 3.7.23.

Yājñavalkya answers Gārgī:

(8) The eighth question, again was by Gārgī, she demands Yājñavalkya to name that which is above the sky, under the earth, in-between the sky and the earth and that covers past, future and present. Yājñavalkya replies that it was 'space'. And when Gārgī further insisted, Yājñavalkya concluded that was the Imperishable (*akṣara*) and says:

That, O Gārgī, brahmaṇas call the Imperishable (*akṣara*). It is not coarse, not fine, not short, not long, not glowing (like fire), not adhesive (like water), without shadow, and without darkness, without air and without space, without stickiness (intangible) odourless, tasteless, without eye, without ear, without voice, without mind, without energy, without breath, without mouth (without personal or family name, un-ageing, undying, without fear immortal, stainless not uncovered), without measure, without inside and without outside.[11]

Further, Yājñavalkya, continues to tell that at the command of the Imperishable, the sun and the moon, the earth and the sky stand apart; days and months, seasons and years happen, and the rivers flow. He says that the performance of sacrifices, worship, and austerity for thousands of years is waste, if one does not know the Imperishable. He repeats again that *Brahman* is beyond our knowledge as earlier said to Uddālaka Āruṇi.

(9) During this discussion to the ninth question raised by Vidagdha Śākalya, Yājñavalkya says that there are three hundred and three, and three thousand and three gods (= 3306).

ŚAṄKARĀCĀRYA'S COMMENTARY

Śaṅkarācārya examined the dialogue between Yājñavalkya and Gārgī that took place twice in the series of discussions held in

11. *Bṛhadāraṇyaka Upaniṣad*, 3.8.8.

the court of king Janaka and has made the following remarks.[12] This dialogue helps to understand that from the earth to space all elements in the world were interlinked, likewise the soul in man is the same as the inner-controller of the universe. Thus this discourse leads to the theory of non-dualism (Advaita) that was very much established in the Upaniṣads.

Śaṅkarācārya also remarks that water is the most important element in the world, which binds all elements of the earth. Śaṅkara believes that the five elements and various worlds have been created for the sake of man. He points out that *Brahman*-knowledge cannot be known through questions and inference, as it is evident from Yājñavalkya's rejection of further questions by Gārgī about divinity. Accordingly Śaṅkara says that the nature and existence of *Brahman* is known from scriptures but not from logic or disputations.[13]

While commenting on the second question of Gārgī about the ultimate ground of the world as the Imperishable *Brahman*, Śaṅkarācārya maintains that there has been a creator of the sun and the moon for lightening the day and night, similar to the maker for the existence of every lamp. Heaven, earth and the rotations of planets have been kept in order by the Imperishable, a ruler in transcendence. The Creator, the Imperishable, as an accountant who calculates income and expenditure carefully, controls the division of time and the course of the rivers. Thus Śaṅkara explains the cosmological argument to prove the existence of the Imperishable, *Brahman* as the universal ruler.[14]

Śaṅkarācārya argues further about the existence of God. He points out that though nobody knows about the results of sacrifice, believing the blessings of God the sacrificer gives away gifts to the priests. If God does not exist the practice of giving gifts might have been discontinued long back. Thus the existence of God cannot be denied.

---

12. *Bṛhadāraṇyaka Upaniṣad Bhāṣya*, 3.6; 3.8.1-12.
13. *Ibid.*, 3.6.
14. *Ibid.*, 3.8.2.

In this context, Śaṅkarācārya analyses the relevance of rituals and God. If rituals and sacrifices yield results when divine affiliation lacks, there shall not be any worship and sacrifices to God. Śaṅkara says that mere performance of sacrifices and ritual does not yield any effects; they are to be performed with the divine knowledge of God. The performance of rituals and sacrifices, practice of austerity are mere waste, if one does not know God. The knowledge of God leads to the cessation of suffering. The performer of sacrifices and rituals, who does not know the knowledge of *Brahman* attains life after life and will get rebirth. A man who dies after knowing the Immutable will become the knower of *Brahman*.[15]

In this context Śaṅkara writes about *Brahman* elaborately. He says that the Imperishable cannot be the insentient *pradhāna* nor anything else and states:

> The *Brahman* which is immediate and direct, which is the self with in all and is beyond the relative attributes of hunger etc., and by which the (un-manifested) ether is pervaded, is the extreme limit, the ultimate goal, the supreme *Brahman*, the truth of truth (the elements) beginning with earth and ending with ether.[16]

The Imperishable *Brahman* perceives, listens, thinks, knows everything and remains a witness. The Imperishable *Brahman* is beyond limiting adjuncts. It is the individual self, *ātma*. It is beyond our thinking and speech. One cannot assert what *Brahman* is, but can assert what that does not *Brahman*. Thus *Brahman* is spoken as 'not this, not this'. In this context Śaṅkarācārya quoted a number of Upaniṣadic sentences. He writes that *Brahman* is

> by nature Pure-Intelligence, homogeneous like a lump of salt. The unconditioned Self, being beyond speech and mind, undifferentiated and one, is designated as 'Not this, not this'. . . The same Self, as by nature

15. *Bṛhadāraṇyaka Upaniṣad Bhāṣya*, 3.8.10.
16. *Ibid.*, 3.8.11.

transcendent, absolute and pure, is called the Immutable and supreme Self.[17]

When we conceive *Brahman* with limiting adjuncts, it is called the internal ruler or *Īśvara* or *saguṇa* Brahma. Śaṅkara says:

> When It has the limiting adjuncts of the body and organs, which are characterised by ignorance, desire and work, It is called the transmigrating individual self. . . . Having the limiting adjuncts of the bodies and organs of *Hiraṇyagarbha*, the Undifferentiated, the gods, the species, the individual, men, animals, spirits, etc., the Self assumes those particular names and forms.[18]

Following are the many sentences of the Upaniṣads asserting the non-duality of the individual self (*ātma*) and the supreme Self (*Brahman*):

— 'The self is *Brahman*' — *Bṛhadāraṇyaka Upaniṣad*, 2.5.19.

— 'This is yourself (that is with in all)' — *Bṛhadāraṇyaka Upaniṣad*, 3.4.1-2; 3.5.1

— 'He is the inner-self of all beings' — *Muṇḍaka Upaniṣad*, 2.1.4.

— 'This (self) being hidden in all beings, etc.' — *Kaṭha Upaniṣad*, 3.12

— 'Thou art That' — *Chāndogya Upaniṣad*, 6.8.7

— 'I, myself, am all this' — *Chāndogya Upaniṣad*, 7.25.1

— 'All this is, but the Self' — *Chāndogya Upaniṣad*, 7.25.2.

---

17. *Bṛhadāraṇyaka Upaniṣad Bhāṣya*, 3.8.12.
18. *Ibid.*

8

Śaṅkarācārya on the Bhagavad Gītā

Introduction

THE *Bhagavad Gītā* means the 'Song of God'. It is a part of the Bhīṣma Parva of the *Mahābhārata*. It contains 700 *śloka*s divided into 18 chapters. For the first time in 1785, Charles Wilkins has translated the *Gītā* into English language.

This song-message has a story in the background. A Great War between Pāṇḍavas and Kauravas at Kurukṣetra took place. In the beginning Arjuna was not interested in war as it results in loss of lives, relatives and social structure. Lord Kṛṣṇa, being the charioteer, told Arjuna to stand up and fight. In his message, Lord Kṛṣṇa analyses all norms, ideas, doctrines, and systems and synthesises them. Arjuna agreed, at last in the end, to perform his duty, *dharma*. Lord Kṛṣṇa's teachings as handed down by tradition have formed the nucleus of the *Gītā*. In the *Bhagavad Gītā*, Kṛṣṇa has been projected as God or incarnation (*avatāra*) of God, the Supreme Being descended upon earth in human form, addressing all men through Arjuna.

It is interpreted that the chief message of the *Gītā* is: 'Do your duty and leave rest to the God'. The *Gītā* in 18.66 records as follows:

> Abandoning all righteous deeds seek me as thy sole refuge;
> I will liberate thee from all sins, do thou not grieve.

Edgerton, a translator of the *Gītā*, writes: 'The *Pithy Anustubh* verses, the flow of the lines, the similes, metaphors — these give it a form, the interest of which cannot be had in any dry analytical philosophical disquisition'. S. Radhakrishnan says that, in the *Gītā* 'We have an interview between God & man. It is the best introduction to Indian Thought & Culture'. The *Gītā* teaches *niṣkāma karma yoga* for Tilak, *anāśakti yoga* and *saṁnyāsa* for Mahatma Gandhi, *karma yoga* for Sri Aurobindo and 'Renunciation' (*tyāga*) according to Śrī Rāmakr̥ṣṇa Paramahaṁsa.

Concepts of the Gītā

LORD KR̥ṢṆA

In the *Bhagavad Gītā*, it is spoken that, Lord Kr̥ṣṇa is the 'Eternal seed of all beings', *bījam mam sarvabhūtānam.* He is the source, sustainer, and destroyer of the world, *jagat*. He is the Imperish able, *akṣara*, and Knower of the field, *kṣetrajña* or the beings in the world of everyday living. The Lord is the Perfect-man, *puruṣottama* and pervades all things, supports all things and 'same to all beings', *samoham sarvabhūteṣu.* The Lord is the father to the creation, *pitā huṁ asya jagato* and dwells in all souls. The Lord God grants the highest goal, *mokṣa* to women, śūdras, vaiśyas. He praises those who see equally a cow, a brāhmaṇa, a dog and a dog-eater. Thus the *Gītā* describes the Lord Kr̥ṣṇa as the goal, supporter, lord, witness, abode, refuge, friend, origin, dissolution, substratum, storehouse, immutable seed.

MAN

According to the *Gītā*, man is a mere instrument, *nimitta-mātra*. Thus the theory of divine pre-destination has been asserted. The *Gītā* says that the three *guṇa*s (qualities) cause every man's way of life:

1. *Sattva* (goodness) — purity, reason, knowledge
2. *Rajas* (passion) — desire, active, restless
3. *Tamas* (dullness) — ignorance, laziness, reverse

The three qualities direct one's existence and thought. They exist in human nature like strands in a twisted rope; and whenever one prevails over the other two, the attitude of a person is tempered by the dominant quality.

The ideal man described in the *Gītā* is the *sthitaprajña* (Man of steadfast-wisdom). The *sthitarajña* is a wise man with equanimity, withdraws his senses from the worldly-objects. He is the self-controlled person, free from desire and pleasure, equally sees the gold and lump of the earth, neither rejoice nor laments, seeks the welfare of all. The man of steadfast-wisdom neither hates nor desires, but remains neutral. No desires overcome him, just as the sea does not overflow though all rivers flow into it. He holds everything equal; and such a man is firm, fearless, self-restrained and dearer to God. However, if we perceive with a research mind, the word courage (*dhīra*) also seems to be one of the ideals that the *Gītā* proposes as the word occurs more times than any concept discussed.

NIṢKĀMA-KARMA-YOGA

The concept of *niṣkāma-karma-yoga* (Discipline of action without desire for the fruits) is the most outstanding teaching upheld by the *Gītā*, which has been universally accepted. The *Gītā* describes *yoga* as a discipline or method by which man's union with God is possible. The extinction of the ego, false self is possible through *yoga*. A man of *yoga* no longer bound with the limitations of body. Action with self-purification leads to *nirvāṇa*. Transcending the normal state of life is the goal of man, according to *Gītā*. It is to become *Brahman*, *brahmābhyām*, and attaining God's presence in one self. In other words, it is the extinction in *Brahman*, *brahma nirvāṇa*. The *Gītā* says that the 'man of steadfast wisdom' attains the *brahma nirvāṇa*.

Paths of the Gītā

KARMA-YOGA (THE DISCIPLINE OF ACTION)

The Discipline of Action (*karma-yoga*) is one of the doctrines of the *Gītā* that insists the performance of actions with balance-mind. It is a 'golden-mean' between attitudes of *pravr̥tti* and *nivr̥tti* (action and withdrawal). Those who are beyond 'faintheartedness' (*hṛdaya-daurbalyam*) can opt for the Path of Action. *Karma-yoga* insists actions (*dharmas*), duties of caste and state. The social obligations are to be discharged, as described by Lord Kṛṣṇa to Arjuna. He also warns that one should not follow others' duty. It is also maintained that the uniqueness of the theory of action is that actions are to be performed without desire for results (*niṣkāma-karma-yoga*).

JÑĀNA-YOGA (THE DISCIPLINE OF KNOWLEDGE)

The Discipline of Knowledge insists upon the knowledge of the self (soul) and purity. *Jñāna-yoga* insists self-control and renunciation and the performance of actions with knowledge. According to the *Gītā*, *jñāna-yoga* leads to absence of conceit, pride and vanity; and asserts forgiveness. A *jñānī* (wise) is one who perceives the self in all and all in the self. He does not give up normal activities of life, but acts for the welfare of the world (*loka-saṁgraha*). The *Gītā* declares that every person attains supreme peace by the highest knowledge: '*karma* creates bondage, *jñāna* liberates from *saṁsāra*'.

BHAKTI-YOGA (THE DISCIPLINE OF DEVOTION)

Bhakti means 'belief in God' or taking refuge in God. The twelfth chapter of the *Gītā* deals with the path of devotion (*bhakti-yoga*). A devotee is satisfied soul and dearer to God; he possesses steadfast wisdom, controlled-mind, beyond praise and suffering. The devotee neither desires nor hates. He is fearless and does not possess egoism; he is self-restrained, pure, adept and silent. He does not hate but compassionate to others. He is of firm conviction, hopes for nothing and is content with whatever comes to him. He neither disturbs the world nor is disturbed by it. According to the *Gītā* devotion to God is essential; consequently liberation comes. Accordingly the *Gītā* declares: 'Abandon all duties, take shelter in God.

YOGA (THE DISCIPLINE OF MEDITATION)

Yoga is used in different ways in the *Gītā*. Fundamentally discipline in action is *yoga*, *karmasu kauśalyam yoga*. *Yoga* insists on self-control and tranquillity. It is a method intends to the control of body, mind and breath. In order to do *yoga*, (*i*) one has to sit in a calm and quite place on the grass/deer-skin, (*ii*) see the tip of nose and (*iii*) keep the mind on one point, that aimed. It is said that *yoga* gives pleasure more than that derived from senses, *yoga* leads to perfect peace and thereby *nirvāṇa* in God.

Kṣetra and kṣetrajña

> *kṣetra jñānam cāpi mam vidhi sarvakṣetresu, bharata,*
> *kṣetra kṣetrajña yor jñānam yat, taj jñānam matam mam.*
> — *Bhagavad Gītā* 13.2

> And do thou also know Me as *kṣetrajña* in all *kṣetras*, O Bharata. The knowledge of *kṣetra* and *kṣetrajña* is deemed by Me as the knowledge.[1]

CONTEXT[2]

The *Bhagavad Gītā* contains a graphic description of the effects of war as perceived by a sensitive person, Arjuna. On Arjuna's request, his chariot was placed between the two armies, then he requested Kṛṣṇa that he did not foresee any advantage in killing one's own people (*sva-jana*).[3] Arjuna stated that he did not desire victory, kingdom or pleasure, for they would mean nothing after the death of one's own people. Arjuna concluded that it would be better for him if the other side kills him while he remains unresisting and unarmed.[4] In His reply Kṛṣṇa expressed His surprise over Arjuna's depression, He exhorted Arjuna not to yield to impotence but get rid of the petty weakness of heart

1. The translation and Śaṅkarācārya's Commentary are from Allādi Mahādeva Śāstrī, tr., *The Bhagavad Gītā with the Commentary of Śrī Śaṅkarācārya*, 1977, pp. 316-35.
2. Adopted from P. George Victor, *Social Philosophy of Vedānta*, 1991.
3. *Bhagavad Gītā*, 1.28. All the references related to the text and commentary are from Allādi Mahādeva Śāstrī, tr., *The Bhagavad Gītā, with the Commentary of Śrī Śaṅkarācārya*, 1977.
4. *The Bhagavad Gītā, with the Commentary of Śrī Śaṅkarācārya*, 2.2, 3.

(*hṛdaya daurbalyam*), and to stand up and fight. In response, Arjuna replied that it was better to live as a beggar than to kill teachers and elders, and to enjoy food smeared with blood. Confessing that he was overcome by commiseration and confused about his duty, he begged Kṛṣṇa to tell him with certainty which was better. He acknowledged himself as disciple of Kṛṣṇa and surrendered and requested Him to teach.[5]

In its thirteenth chapter, the *Bhagavad Gītā* states that the body is called the field (*kṣetra*) and the Supreme Lord, who knows it, is called the knower of the field (*kṣetrajña*).[6] The body is the field, which consists of elements, self-sense (*ahaṁkāra*), understanding, un-manifest, the ten senses, mind and the five objects of the senses along with its modifications. The mental traits also belong to the body.[7] The knower of the field (*kṣetrajña*) with His hands, feet, ears and eyes everywhere encompasses all things in the world. He is described in a series of paradoxes. He seems to have the qualities of all the senses and yet free from all the senses, unattached and yet supporting all. He is free from the qualities (*guṇa*s) and yet enjoying them, outside the beings yet within them, unmoving yet moving, far away yet near, undivided yet seem to be divided. Thus, He lies behind all active states and the world as a witness. He is the Light of lights and beyond darkness. There is no knowledge without Him and He is the object and goal of knowledge. Further it is said that He dwells in the heart of every being.[8]

COMMENTARY

Śaṅkarācārya has interpreted the doctrine of the true nature of *kṣetra* and *kṣetrajña*. He gives the following meanings to the words *kṣetra* and *kṣetrajña*:

---

5. *The Bhagavad Gītā*, 2.7.
6. *Ibid.*, 13.1.
7. *Ibid.*, 13.5, 6.
8. *Ibid.*, 13.13-17.

kṣetra	=	the field, the body, the matter, all the knowable.
kṣetrajña	=	knower of the field, comprehender of matter, cogniser, understander, *Īśvara*.

Lord Kṛṣṇa proclaims himself as the knower of the field, body (*kṣetrajña*) and dwells in all bodies (*kṣetra*s). Śaṅkarācārya writes that to perceive the supreme Lord, firstly, as 'One exists in all beings' and secondly as the 'Knower of all things and beings' are the main objectives of true knowledge.

Śaṅkarācārya writes that nothing exists apart from the creator and sustainer of the world, *Īśvara*. *Īśvara* is *kṣetrajña* or knower of the field (body), and exists in all beings. In his usual nature Śaṅkara raises doubts and thereby gives an explanation. If *Īśvara* lives in all bodies, it would follow that *Īśvara* experience what the body experiences. In other words, the opponents of Vedānta say that *Īśvara* is a *saṁsārin* as he exists in all *kṣetra*s. Śaṅkara rejects this viewpoint and asserts that *saṁsāra* (family life) pertains to the body and sense-organs only but not to *kṣetrajña*, *Īśvara*. Attributes like pleasure, pain, desire and hatreds are related to the *kṣetra* (body) but they do not actually pertain to the Self or *kṣetrajña* or *Īśvara*.[9] *Saṁsāra* which consists in doing and enjoying life in this world, is attributed to the self due to ignorance born of *tamas* (darkness). Likewise a man who is affected with the *timira* disease to the eyes perceives things in a different way, similarly due to the veil of ignorance one perceives the *kṣetrajña* as a *saṁsārin*. When *timira* is removed by treatment of the eye, the patient perceives clearly. Similarly false perception and doubt are related to the sense-organs but not to the *kṣetrajña*.[10] When knowledge downs ignorance ceases.

---

9. Allādi Mahādeva Śāstrī, *op. cit.*, p. 322.
10. *Ibid.*, p. 324.

Therefore, the conclusion is that ignorance is related to body, but not to the self, and the *saṁsāra* is to the *kṣetra* (body) but not to the *kṣetrajña* (knower). *Saṁsāra* is based upon ignorance (*avidyā*).

On the bases of the denial of *saṁsāra* to the self, the opponents of Vedānta would say that there is no need of śāstras (scriptures). But Śaṅkara says that śāstras (scriptures) have a purpose to serve for those who are in the state of bondage but not to those in the state of liberation.[11] Prohibitions and injunctions of the śāstra do not apply to him who knows the Self. Those who realise the identity of the individual self and *Brahman* are beyond *dharma* and *adharma* of *saṁsāra* (family life). The aim of life in this world is to realise the unity of self and *Brahman*. It is called liberation and possible in this very life. Such a man who attains liberation in this world is not afraid of anything. He does not engage in actions (*karma*s).[12]

In this connection, Śaṅkarācārya warns against false teachers or a class of *paṇḍit*s, who say that body itself is the Self and also others who say that the individual self is different from the Supreme Self and through meditation one can attain the state of the true nature of God, *Īśvara*. According to Śaṅkara these are the people who speak themselves as the traditional (*sampradāya*) *paṇḍit*s of the śāstras, but in actuality they are not, but ignorant.[13]

For Allādi Mahādeva Śāstrī, Śaṅkara's commentary contains the following main points:

1. The body and self are different.
2. The self is the Supreme Self.
3. Due to ignorance the self is subjected to evil, rites and *saṁsāra*.

---

11. Allādi Mahādeva Śāstrī, *op. cit.*, p. 325.
12. *Ibid.*, p. 328.
13. *Ibid.*, p. 330.

4. The body (*kṣetra*) is unaffected by *saṁsāra*, the family life in the world.
5. Ignorance (*avidyā*) is an inherent property of body, not the self.
6. Scriptural injunctions apply only to the state of bondage, and concerned with ignorants.
7. The relation of the Self to *saṁsāra* is a mere illusion.
8. The relation of ignorance to the Self is also a mere illusion.[14]

Śaṅkarācārya has explicitly discussed the role of *avidyā* (ignorance) in relation to person in his commentary. He says that because of *avidyā* (ignorance), *saṁsāra* (family life, which consists of duties and suffering) is attributed to the Self. *Avidyā* arises due to *tamas*. Śaṅkarācārya says:

> As partaking of the nature of a veil, *avidya* whether causing perception of what is quite the contrary of truth, or causing doubt, or causing nescience or non-perception of a truth is a *tamasic* notion, i.e., a notion born of *tamas*. For, on the dawn of the light of discrimination, it disappears.[15]

Therefore, it is to be noted that *avidyā* is not the property of the self, cogniser. *Avidyā* makes man not to apprehend the truth, reality and right, like the *timira* (an eye disease) which causes dimness of sight. *Avidyā* is a kind of veil that covers cognition and perception of man. Whenever *timira* is removed by the treatment of the eye, one can see clearly; similarly, the cessation of *avidyā* leads to right understanding and clear cognition. According to Advaita Vedānta, bondage of the self to the world is due to *avidyā*. Whenever *avidyā* is removed, man gets liberation from bondage. Bondage and liberation are opposed to each other. The existence of *avidyā* is known from the action and rites one commits. *Avidyā* is a mistaken notion and can be perceived from the one who has the *avidyā*.

---

14. These are the sub-headings given by Allādi Mahādeva Śāstrī to the commentary of Śaṅkara.
15. *Ibid*., p. 323.

According to the Vedānta scriptures, the ignorant man who does not know the self experiences calamity. He lives a life of the blind lead by another blind man. According to the *Bṛhadāraṇyaka Upaniṣad* a man who thinks himself different from *Brahman* becomes a beast for the Gods. He regards the physical body as the self, and performs *dharma* and *adharma*. The ignorant lead by attachment and other evil passions, but do not follow the wise. They practice all sorts of actions and black-magic and believe the world, as it appears to them. In this commentary Śaṅkarācārya concludes that though *Īśvara* exists in all beings, He is not affected by the pain and pleasures of *saṁsāra* as *Īśvara* is different from the body. Śaṅkara asserts that scriptures have a purpose with reference to the ignorant people and the injunctions apply to the state of bondage.

Abandonment and seeking the Lord as shelter

sarva dharmān parityajya māmekam śaraṇam vraja
aham tva sarva pāpābhyo mokṣayisyāmi, mā sucaḥ.
— *Bhagavad Gītā*, 18.66

Abandoning all righteous deeds, seek me as they sole Refuge;

I will liberate thee from all sins, do thou not grieve.[16]

COMMENTARY[17]

Fundamentally, the poem represents four conceptions:

1. Renunciation of all deeds
2. Seek God as the only refuge, shelter
3. Cessation of *saṁsāra,* and
4. Attainment of the Highest Bliss (*mokṣa*).

---

16. Alladi Mahādeva Śāstrī, *op. cit.*, pp. 499-516.
17. This commentary of Śaṅkara exclusively summarises the words and phrases of the *Bhagavad Gītā*, thus differs from other commentaries of Śaṅkara. However, the spirit is the same to that of Advaita message.

The verse is profound, because it envisages the message and essence of the Vedānta texts. The word *sarva-dharma* indicates both lawful and unlawful actions. In the *Bhagavad Gītā* the word *mokṣa* (liberation) has been indicated with different words such as *nis-śreyasa* and *kaivalya*.[18] Śaṅkarācārya writes that 'renunciation of all actions' (*naiṣkarmya*) is necessary to attain the self-knowledge, which provides liberation (*mokṣa*). This commentary of Śaṅkara exclusively summarises the verses of the *Bhagavad Gītā* and differs from other commentaries. However the spirit is the same to that of Advaita doctrines.

The commentary of Śaṅkara discusses the means to attain the highest bliss (*nis-śreyasa*) or liberation (*mokṣa*). The answer contains with the following viewpoints:

1. Self-knowledge alone leads to liberation, the Highest Bliss.
2. Actions (*karma*s) should not be associated with knowledge.
3. There is no liberation through actions.
4. The path of knowledge and the path of action are meant for the wise and ignorant respectively.
5. Actions are based upon ignorance (*avidyā*).
6. The Self is different from the body and does not connected with its actions, and their connected results.

Śaṅkarācārya in his commentary says that the realisation of the individual self as the Supreme Self is liberation (*mokṣa*). It is the highest bliss, and possible when ignorance (*avidyā*) is removed by knowledge of the Self. *Avidyā* consists of identifying the self with body and the actions associated with it. Man considers himself as the agent and enjoyer of actions due to false identification, in the form of 'I am the agent, I do this act for such and such a result'.[19] It can be compared to mistaking a rope

---

18. Allādi Mahādeva Śāstrī, *op. cit.*, p. 500.
19. *Ibid.*

as serpent in the darkness. This error is removed whenever the light comes.

It is also said that the identification of body and self is a *mithyā-pratyaya* (illusory notion) but not *gauṇa-pratyaya* (figurative expression). A figurative expression is that where similarity is taken to extol the subject. For example, the expressions 'Devadatta is a lion' and the 'The student is fire' are intended to express the resemblance of lion and fire with respect to Devadatta and the student. One knows that in reality Devadatta is neither a lion nor the student is fire, but it is merely intended to indicate the wild nature of Devadatta and the yellow colour of the student. Contrary to this *gauṇa-pratyaya* (figurative expression), the *mithyā-pratyaya* (illusory notion) is that where distinction between two things is not perceived. For instance, in darkness when a pillar is mistaken for a man, there is lack of distinction; and similarly the body is mistaken for the self. This is the effect of an illusory notion (*mithyā-pratyaya*).[20]

The identification of body and self is due to *avidyā* (ignorance). Due to this identification, one is attached to all actions including *dharma* (right) and *adharma* (wrong), and experiences the results of them.[21] The relation between actions and their results forms a cycle of actions and their results extending one birth to the other and from the present to the future. This is *saṁsāra*, which is without beginning and end. When *avidyā* (ignorance) ceases through devotion to knowledge with renunciation of all actions, then *saṁsāra*, which consists of actions and their results, pain and pleasure, will cease.

The Vedic passages assert the performance of actions and describe them as obligatory duties. Performance of actions leads either to heaven or hell, but not *mokṣa*. Though, it is a fact that, actions and knowledge are enjoined, they meant for different classes of people. Śaṅkarācārya says that *avidyā* (ignorance) and *karma* (ritual) constitute the seed of all actions. Therefore action

20. Allādi Mahādeva Śāstrī, *op. cit.*, p. 510.
21. *Ibid.*, p. 511.

relates to the ignorant, while knowledge and renunciation of actions pertain to the wise. The wise identify the self with the Supreme Self and perceive that the self is not the agent; and they devote themselves to the knowledge of the Self and reach the fourth highest order of life, *paramahaṁsa parivrājaka*.[22]

In this connection Śaṅkarācārya has referred to *nitya* (regular), *naimittika* (occasional), *kāmya* (desired) and *prāyaścitta* (expiatory) *karmas*.[23] All these actions concern only him who is ignorant. Though the scriptures enjoin *the nitya karma*s they pertain to the ignorant only. Śaṅkara says that *nitya karma*s are not meant to destroy the past sins, but are just enjoined as man identifies himself with the body. *Nitya karma* is not *prāyaścitta karma*, on the other hand, *nitya karma*s and *kāmya karma*s are almost equal. The performance of both these *karma*s involves trouble and pain equally. The Vedic literature says that the performance of *nitya karma*s produce merit (*puṇya*) as its result. Similarly performance of duties of particular caste and stage leads one to attain happiness.[24]

A passage in this commentary prohibits that neither actions nor the combination of actions and knowledge can lead to knowledge; on the other hand knowledge alone leads one to attain liberation (*mokṣa*).[25] Śaṅkarācārya says that no one follows the path of actions when one is getting liberation through the knowledge as if a man has a choice to choose either a kingdom or a piece of land, certainly he will choose the kingdom.[26] Similarly when a country is full of floods and streams there is no need for constructing tanks and digging wells. So also when knowledge leads to liberation nobody would ever desire or seek to perform any kind of actions, which require money, men, material and co-ordination.

---

22. Allādi Mahādeva Śāstrī, *op.cit.*, 509.
23. Śaṅkara has mentioned about these *karma*s in his commentary to the *Bhagavad Gītā*, 5.13, *ibid.*, pp. 166-7.
24. *Ibid.*, p. 504.
25. *Ibid.*, p. 502.
26. *Ibid.*

It is said that the self is neither the agent nor the enjoyer of the results of the actions performed by the body. Though the self dwells in the body it is untouched by the pain and pleasures of the body. There is a view against Vedāntic view that though the self does not directly engage in actions, by mere presence it becomes an agent. An example is given in this context that though a king or a commander does not engage directly himself in a war, when his soldiers fight, he is said to be victorious or defeated. Thus the king or a commander is connected with results of war. Śaṅkarācārya writes that the king should not be considered as an indirect participant, on the other hand he is a real agent as causing others to fight paying them salaries and reaping the fruits.[27] Therefore he says that the example is unreasonable. As the body and self are distinct in reality, the identification of them is an illusory notion just like in the case of dreams and magic. In deep-sleep, *samādhi*, where there is a break in the continuity of illusory notions, identification of the self with body is impossible. Therefore *saṁsāra* is an illusion as it based upon the illusory identification of self and body. The right knowledge, which makes one to realise the distinction between self and body inturn conduces to the cessation of *saṁsāra*.[28] The essence, in Śaṅkarācārya's words, is this:

> Therefore works are not the means to the Highest Bliss. Neither is a conjunction of knowledge and works possible. Nor can it be held that knowledge, which leads to emancipation, requires the aid of works; for as removing *avidyā*, knowledge is opposed to works. Indeed, darkness cannot remove darkness. Therefore, knowledge alone is the means to the Highest Bliss.[29]

---

27. Allādi Mahādeva Śāstrī, *op.cit.*, p. 515.
28. *Ibid.*, p. 516.
29. *Ibid.*, p. 502.

9

Śaṅkarācārya on the Brahma Sūtra

Bādarāyaṇa

THE *Brahma Sūtra* attributed to Bādarāyaṇa, who is identified with Vedavyāsa by tradition, is the only surviving full-length work, which tries to systematise the philosophical views of the Upaniṣads. Most of the modern critical scholars do not think that the author of the *Brahma Sūtra* and the author of the Itihāsa-Purāṇas are identical, in fact the latter literature has several authors, spread over many centuries. The Japanese scholar Nakamura thinks that Bādarāyaṇa is referred to in the *Brahma Sūtra* like other Mīmāṁsā and Vedānta teachers and is different from its author; but he admits that Śaṅkarācārya acknowledged Bādarāyaṇa as its author.

The *Brahma Sūtra* is the basic text of Vedānta, hence called the *Vedānta-sūtras*. The *Brahma Sūtra* claims to be an inquiry regarding *Brahman*, the world-ground, which is the source of the scriptures and can be known from scriptures through harmonious juxtaposition of the relevant texts. It explains Brahmā as the sole reality. The *Brahma Sūtra* records that Brahmā is real, eternal, omniscient. It teaches about Brahmā, world and soul and brings out the contradictions in the doctrines of opponents.

Regarding the date of the *Brahma Sūtra*, S.L. Pandey and G.C. Pandey are of the opinion that it was composed in-between second century BC and second century AD. But some Indian scholars date it to 500-200 BC. Max-Müller believes that the *Brahma Sūtra* was earlier to the *Gītā*. Nakamura remarks that

AD 400-50 is the period during which time it was compiled in its present form, though many portions of it must have existed earlier. He also thinks that the sections of the Sūtra those directly dealing with Upaniṣadic texts have compiled prior to the Christian era. The chief points of the *Brahma Sūtra* are the following:

1. *Brahman* is the sole reality.
2. *Brahman* is the world-ground and source of the scriptures and can be known from scriptures.
3. Veda is eternal and man has no right to question the authority of the Veda.
4. Scriptures are authority and the Upaniṣads uphold Śruti and Smṛti.
5. Logic (*tarka*) is not useful to know metaphysical truths.

The *Brahma Sūtra* contains 555 *sūtra*s. A *sūtra* consists of 2 or 3 words each and is an aphoristic phrase, designed to remind the essence of a doctrine and reflects the oral tradition of ancient times. The *Brahma Sūtra* is divided into 4 chapters.

SAMANVAYA (RECONCILIATION OF DIFFERENT STATEMENTS)

In this chapter Bādarāyaṇa remarks that the perception of seers is based on their personal and religious experiences, hence, contradictory assertions arise. Therefore, different Vedāntic statements are to be reconciled in order to establish the theory of *Brahman*. Even in the Upaniṣads *Brahman* or *ātman* is mentioned; sometimes *ākāśa* and *prāṇa* have been referred to *Brahman*. Therefore the meaning of the term should be taken on the basis of the context in which it is used. In this chapter, an account of the nature of *Brahman*, its relation with world and *ātman* has been discussed.

AVIRODHA (OPPONENT'S VIEW CRITICISED)

In this second chapter, which means 'non-conflict', Bādarāyaṇa discusses the objections brought by opponents against the

Vedāntic view and criticised the rival theories. Sāṁkhya system proposes *pradhāna* or *prakṛti* as the cause of world-evolution. This standpoint has been rejected, by stating that the inert and un-intelligent *pradhāna* cannot be the base and source for the designed and planned world. The Vaiśeṣikas argue that primary atoms are the basis for the world, and remarks that the *adraṣṭa* (unseen) power is responsible for bringing the atoms together for the creation of the world. How the unseen potency moves the atoms have no answer in their explanations. The Buddhists proposed the doctrine of momentariness; but they have not resolved how these successive moments are related. Bādarāyaṇa, in the later part of this chapter discusses the status of the individual soul's and its relation to Absolute God; the world's dependence on Absolute God, *Brahman* has been noted.

SĀDHANA (MEANS)

This third chapter contains the ways and means to obtain *Brahman* knowledge. An account of the doctrine of rebirth maintained. For Cārvākas there is no soul apart from the body. If it is the case why the dead body does not move and have consciousness — is the question raised by Bādarāyaṇa. He maintains that there are two paths: *deva-yāna* and *pitṛ-yāna* (the path of gods and the path of fathers). If a person follows meditation and *Brahman* knowledge, the soul goes to *Brahma-loka;* and if the person performs sacrifices the soul goes to *pitṛ-yāna.* Those who does not fit to these two paths are bound to born again and again as tiny beings and die again and again. This chapter elaborately discusses the process of the doctrine of rebirth and migration of the souls.

PHALA (FRUIT, RESULT)

In this last chapter of the *Brahma Sūtra*, Bādarāyaṇa has brought out the following points:

(i) Fruit of *Brahman* knowledge.
(ii) Departure of the soul after death.
(iii) The path of gods and the path of fathers.
(iv) Nature of liberation.

Bādarāyaṇa brings in this chapter the unique perspective of the Advaita, which asserts that the one who follows the path of knowledge attains liberation in this very life. *Brahman* realisation is nothing but freedom from all sins; and the liberated one is called the *jīvan-mukta.*

Bādarāyaṇa, in the *Brahma Sūtra*, maintains the *saguṇa* and *nirguṇa* perspectives of Brahma, the identity of *Brahman* and *ātman* and the important two paths of transmigration as brought out by Śaṅkarācārya in his Advaita Vedānta. According to S. Radhakrishnan 'the vagueness of the Upaniṣad view of creation remains in it'. The unique proposition of the *Brahma Sūtra* is that apart from the three upper castes, who are entitled to perform sacrifice, the śūdras and women attain salvation through the grace of God.

Superimposition (adhyāsa)[1]

In his commentary on the *Brahma Sūtra*, at the beginning of its first chapter, called reconciliation (*samanvaya*), Śaṅkarācārya analyses about superimposition (*adhyāsa*).

Generally in our daily life, we see how certain people impose their own ideas on others or assert their ideas as the ideas of all people as a whole. In other words, a person states his words and ideas as the ideas and words of the people in the society. Likewise some people assert the ideas of them as the ideas of others. For example, among a group of students, if a student says 'let us have a cup of tea', it means actually that the student is interested in tea. But he imposed his preference over the others, therefore he leads them to take tea. Another example may also be taken for clear understanding. In a statement of a husband, 'Let us go to the park', the word 'us' represents both the husband and his wife, but actually the husband imposes his preference over the wife instead of saying 'I prefer to go to park'. This is a kind of

1. The summaries of Śaṅkarācārya's commentary are based upon Swāmī Gambhīrānanda, tr., *Brahma-Sūtra-Bhāṣya of Śrī Śaṅkarācārya*, 1977.

superimposition similar to what Śaṅkarācārya interpreted long ago.

Śaṅkarācārya says that human behaviour is based upon the identification of 'I' and 'we' due to lack of discrimination. Men mix up, reality with unreality, i.e., 'I' with 'we'. Śaṅkara brings a discussion of the two words 'I' and 'we' in his commentary to the *Brahma Sūtra* as introduction. Here, 'I' stands for a single person while 'we' represent many persons. Actually the opinion of 'I' exists but not at all the opinion of 'we'. It is due to the superimposition of one's own ideas on the other. Thus 'we' or the opinions of 'we' do not exist but only the 'I'. Hence 'I' is objective while 'we' is subjective. The subject 'we' always represent the attributes of the object 'I'. This is the superimposition of the object 'I' and its attributes on the subject 'we'. Śaṅkara points out that, superimposition is a state of the awareness of mind, which considers one thing as something else. Following are different viewpoints of superimposition (*adhyāsa*) noted by Śaṅkara:

1. Superimposition is a kind of memory arises on the basis of some past experience.
2. Superimposition consists in identifying the attributes of one thing on the other.
3. Superimposition is nothing but confusion due to absence of discrimination between two things.
4. Superimposition is a kind of fancying opposite attributes of a thing to its substratum.[2]

According to Śaṅkarācārya the fundamental feature of superimposition is nothing but considering the appearance of one thing as something else.[3] The example noted by Śaṅkara in this connection is the appearance of nacre as silver. In the similar way, children superimpose the dirt of the earth's surface on the sky. Śaṅkara says that superimposition is neither limited to

---

2. Swāmī Gambhīrānanda, *op. cit.*, p. 2.
3. *Ibid.*, p. 3.

immediately perceived things nor to a particular activity; it pervades the whole activity of life. He says that there is superimposition of non-self on self, which is opposed to it. The important point is that, the characteristics and attributes of the thing superimposed do not affect the locus or the actual thing. According to the wise men of his times, superimposition arises due to ignorance (*avidyā*). And the separation of the superimposed attributes or characteristics from the real thing is *vidyā* (knowledge or enlightenment).

On the basic assumption Śaṅkarācārya says that the whole activity of life, the scriptures, the ritual behaviour, and the means of knowledge like perception is based upon the superimposition of the non-self on the self due to ignorance or *avidyā*.[4] He states that the body, senses and mind are essential for man to become a cogniser. Perception is impossible without senses; and the senses cannot function without a body; and the body cannot function unless the idea of the self is superimposed on it. Thus according to Śaṅkara the means of knowledge and scriptures are based upon man who is subjected to ignorance. Thus Śaṅkara rejects perception and scriptures with reference to empirical things. Śaṅkara asserts that all the Vedic behaviour, performance of rituals presuppose the superimposition of caste, life stage and condition on the self. The Vedic command, which states that a brāhmaṇa has to perform a sacrifice, presupposes various kinds of superimposition of caste, stage and condition on the self. Thus, Śaṅkara rejects perception and scriptures with reference to empirical things. He says that the empirical behaviour of men and animals is same regarding the use of the means of perception.[5] For example, animals run away if they hear frightening sounds or see a man with raised stick in his hand; on the other hand, they come near to a man with green grass in his hands. Similarly human beings avert to frightening noises or dangerous people with swords in their hands.

Simply speaking superimposition means 'the cognition of

---

4. Swāmī Gambhīrānanda, *op. cit.*, p. 4.
5. *Ibid.*, p. 5.

something as some other thing'. If any relative of a family suffers from loss of any limb in an accident, one says 'I myself injured'. Sometime's man superimposes the characteristics of the body on the self. When a man thinks that he is fat or lean, he is attributing the qualities of the body on his self. Like that when a man thinks that he is deaf or dumb he is attributing the qualities of his senses to the self. In the same way man superimposes the internal organ, the idea of ego on the self, which is the witness of everything and which is opposed to non-self. Śaṅkarācārya says that the self is free from caste differences, bodily cravings and feelings. The knowledge of the self is opposed to scriptural duties because all scriptural duties are prior to the rise of the knowledge of the self.

Thus superimposition is natural and appears to be beginning less and endless. It is the source of all evils, Śaṅkara says that for the removal of it and for attaining the knowledge of the unity of the self, the study of Vedānta has begun and has been explained.

THE FIRST BRAHMA SŪTRA

athāto brahma jijñāsā

(Prerequisites for the Knowledge of *Brahman*)

atha	=	Then
ataḥ	=	Therefore
brahma jijñāsā	=	Enquiry into *Brahman*.

Then, therefore, an enquiry into (the nature of) *Brahman*.

Bādarāyaṇa has written the *Brahma Sūtra* (aphorisms) to synthesise the knowledge of *Brahman* expressed in the Upaniṣads. As each aphorism (*sūtra*) contains only few words, to understand its meaning has become difficult in later times, hence Śaṅkarācārya wrote a commentary by giving the right meaning to the words of each aphorism (*sūtra*) of Bādarāyaṇa.

In his commentary, firstly, Śaṅkarācārya says that in this aphorism the word *atha* (then) is used possibly to indicate the study of the Upaniṣads. It does not mean the study of the Vedas, because the knowledge of *dharma* (religious action) depends upon the study of the Vedas. While the performance of religious actions results in secular prosperity, the knowledge of *Brahman* leads to liberation (*mokṣa*). Therefore, Śaṅkara says that the knowledge of *Brahman* does not depend on either religious actions or human effort.[6] He says that the word *atha* (then) indicates certain practices as prerequisites (*sādhanā catuṣṭaya*) for the knowledge of *Brahman*. They are:

(i) Discrimination between what is eternal and what is non-eternal.

(ii) Renunciation of all desires to enjoy the results of ones' actions in this world and hereafter.

(iii) Development of a perfect personality by controlling mind, sense organs, etc.

(iv) The desire for liberation.[7]

Secondly, Śaṅkarācārya observes that the word *ataḥ* (therefore) indicates a consequence. According to him, *ataḥ* is nothing but the need to study *Brahman*-knowledge which is the only way to attain the highest goal, liberation. Through the study of the Vedas and performance of actions one may attain enjoyable things or higher things but not the highest human goal, liberation.

Thirdly, Śaṅkarācārya says that the word *Brahman* should not be mistaken for brāhmaṇa caste. *Brahman* is the source and sustainer of the beings and the world. If *Brahman* is known everything will be known, because it is the basis and cause of everything. For example, if one knows what gold is, then every ornament that is made of gold is known. He gives an example of a king in this regard. The statement 'There goes the king' implies that the king is going along with his ministers and aids.[8] In the

6. Swāmī Gambhīrānanda, *op. cit.*, p. 8.
7. *Ibid.*, p. 9.
8. *Ibid.*, p. 11.

similar way, the study of the knowledge of *Brahman* implies all the subsidiary things that are to be known.

Lastly, Śaṅkarācārya points out that *brahma-jijñāsā* is essential to learn as a number of schools have confused the ordinary man. The materialists (lokāyatas) and others have confused the people by their opposite and contradictory doctrines and ways. According to the doctrines of lokāyata the body alone is the self and others maintaining that mind is the self or takes momentary-consciousness or void for self. Again some say that the self is an agent and enjoyer, and for others it is not. In this connection, Śaṅkara asserts that if one follows some view or the other, it leads one into sorrow and prevents him from attaining liberation. Therefore it is essential to ascertain the right meaning of the passages of the Upaniṣads and *Brahma-sūtra* to help the people for attaining liberation (*mokṣa*). Thus the study of *Brahman*-knowledge is essential.

THE SECOND BRAHMA SṛTRA

janmadasya yataḥ
(*Brahman* is the Creator)

janma	=	Birth (origin)
ādi =	etc.	
asya	=	of this (world)
yataḥ	=	from which

From this, birth (origin) and, etc., of this (world) proceed.

According to Śaṅkarācārya, the phrase *janma-ādi* (origin, etc.) indicates the sustenance and dissolution of the world. It is because some passages of the Upaniṣads state the order of the nature of things where origin, sustenance and dissolution are mentioned. The word, *asya* (of this) indicates what is perceived immediately by us through perception. Thus the word *asya* or 'of this' refer to the world around us. The next word of the aphorism *yataḥ* (from which) implies the cause, which is *Brahman*. Following this the meaning is that the omniscient and omnipotent *Brahman* is the cause from which the origin (birth), sustenance and dissolution of this world go forth. Śaṅkara says that a number of changes are there in the evolution of a thing from birth to death, but all the modifications are included in the three major changes — origin, sustenance and dissolution. He further clarifies that the world has no other cause for its existence except *Brahman*.

As advocated by the Sāṁkhya School of thought, the *pradhāna* or *prakṛti* is not the cause of this world. The world has not originated spontaneously from its own nature (*svabhāva*) as propounded by the naturalists. Everything that produced depends upon a specific cause, time and place in the world; on this basis the Naiyāyikas or logicians establish the existence of God with reference to the world.[9]

In this connection, Śaṅkarācārya says that the aphorisms are used to infer the existence of God, which differs from transmigrating self. He says that the aphorism is intend to correlate the various sentences of the Upaniṣadic texts, because the realisation of *Brahman* is possible by the assertion and discussion of the meaning of the Vedāntic passages, but not from inference. However, Śaṅkara says that inference is admitted to confirm the meaning of the Vedāntic passages so far as it does not differ from the texts. Some Vedāntic passages also state that human intelligence is helpful in understanding the scriptures. It is said in the *Bṛhadāraṇyaka Upaniṣad* that the self in man is to be heard of and to be reflected upon. The *Chāndogya Upaniṣad* says that only a man who is informed and intelligent and who has been taught by a teacher can know the self.[10]

According to Śaṅkarācārya, the Vedic scriptures and symbols used in them are useful and means to acquire the religious duties. Whereas the Vedāntic texts and personal experience are said to be the valid means of the knowledge of *Brahman*, as the knowledge of *Brahman* culminates in experience of *Brahman* (*brahma-sākṣātkāra*).[11]

---

9. Swāmī Gambhīrānanda, *op. cit.*, pp. 14-15.
10. *Bṛhadāranyaka Upaniṣad*, 2.4.5., *Chāndogya Upaniṣad*. 6.14.2. Cf., R.E. Hume, *The Thirteen Principal Upaniṣad*s, 1949.
11. Swamī Gambhīrānanda, *op. cit.*, p. 16.

Religious actions are related to human effort. The Vedic texts prescribe the rules and methodology of their performance. Actions may be performed or may not be performed or can be done in different ways like a man who wants to go somewhere or to Gāndhāra region can go on foot, or by horse or by a cart. Thus one's choice depends on one's notions. The true knowledge of an existing thing depends on neither human effort nor notion but on the thing in itself. Suppose there is a pillar, the true knowledge of its existence and reality depends on itself, whether one perceives it or not. Like that *Brahman* is an existing one and the true knowledge of it depends on itself. Śaṅkara points out that the senses cannot apprehend *Brahman*, like that of an external thing. The *Taittirīya Upaniṣad* asserts that *Brahman* alone is the cause for the birth, continuation and death of all beings in the world:

> That, verily, whence beings here are born, that by which when born they live, that into which on de-ceasing they enter that be desirous of understanding. That is *Brahman*.[12]

Thus in this aphorism, Śaṅkarācārya proved that *Brahman* is the cause of this world.

THE THIRD BRAHMA SŪTRA

> ***śāstra yonitvāt***
> (Scripture is the Source for *Brahman*)
>
> *śāstra* = Scripture
> *yonitvāt* = being the source
>
> (The omniscience of *Brahman* follows that it is) being the source of scripture.

This aphorism has been understood in two different ways. At first it is explained that *Brahman* is the cause of the scriptures like the *R̥gveda* and, etc. It is said so because scriptures like the *R̥gveda* contains injunctions in favour of good actions, and such

12. *Taittirīya Upaniṣad*, 3.1. Cf., R.E. Hume, *op. cit.*, p. 290.

a good scripture cannot be the product of any one other than the all-knowing *Brahman*. For example, Pāṇini is famous as a grammarian, but his grammar is a part of a subject. The *Ṛg-veda*, which contains all the branches of knowledge, should necessarily be the product of a great Being. Accordingly the *Bṛhadāraṇyaka Upaniṣad* enumerates that the *Ṛgveda* was emanated from the great Being.[13] Thus *Brahman* is the source of scriptures.

The words of the aphorism can also be understood in a different way, as it is not clear. The other explanation is that the scripture is the valid means for knowing *Brahman*. Here the scripture is taken for granted as the real means to attain the knowledge of *Brahman* but not perception or any other means. Śaṅkarācārya says that an object in existence can be perceived by perception; but in the case of *Brahman* direct perception does not give us the knowledge, as *Brahman* is beyond the empirical level. Therefore scripture is the source of *Brahman*.[14]

THE FOURTH BRAHMA SŪTRA

tattu samanvayāt

(Harmonious Juxtaposition of Vedānta Passages)

tat	=	that
tu	=	but
samanvayāt	=	because it is connected as their purport.

But that (*Brahman* is to be known from scriptures) because it is connected (with the Vedānta texts) as their purport.

Śaṅkarācārya wrote an elaborate commentary to the fourth aphorism of the *Brahma Sūtra* written by Bādarāyaṇa. This aphorism contains simply two words, *tattu* and *samanvayāt*. For him the word *tat* (that) indicates *Brahman*. The earlier three aphorisms explain the desire for an inquiry into the nature of

13. Swāmī Gambhīrānanda, *op. cit.*, p. 19.
14. *Ibid.*, pp. 19, 20.

Brahman, as *Brahman* is the cause for the origin, sustenance and dissolution of this world. Therefore the word *tat* (that) is used as a predicate referring to *Brahman*. And the word *tu* (but) is meant to rule out the opposite view (*pūrva-pakṣa*); hence the word *samanvayāt* asserts the reconciliation and comparison of all the Vedānta passages and scriptures.

The commentary contains a number of doubts as expressed by the opponent for which the *advaitin*, Śaṅkarācārya has explained and answered elaborately. The following are the doubts raised by the opponents of Vedānta, termed as the *pūrva-pakṣa* by Śaṅkarācārya:

(1) The opponent says that the Vedas enjoin various actions (*karma*s) to be performed by the individual; so, if it is accepted on the basis of the authority of the Vedas, views against to the performance of actions are useless. On the other hand, it is true that the Upaniṣads do not enjoin *karma*s or duties, therefore they are useless, because they are opposing the authority of the Vedas.

(2) Further the opponent says that if at all the Upaniṣads enjoin anything, it is only meditation (*upāsanā*) which can be considered as action (*karma*). It can also be further stated that if the Upaniṣads speak of a thing, which is already in existence, their purport is useless. In other words, if the Upaniṣads speak of actions, their purpose is waste because, the Vedas have already discussed about the actions (*karma*s).

(3) The opponent says that, in one way the Upaniṣads might be meaningful, i.e., while the Vedas enjoin actions or duties for those who desire heaven, the Upaniṣads enjoin the knowledge of *Brahman* for those who seek liberation (*mokṣa*).

(4) The opponent is also of the opinion that apart from learning scriptures, meditation is also necessary, as the Upaniṣads assert that the self is to be known through hearing, reflection and profound meditation (*śravaṇa*,

manana, and *nididhyāsana*). It is to be noted here that even acquiring knowledge can also be taken as mental action according to the opponent (*pūrva-pakṣa*) viewpoint.

(5) Though the liberation is inherent in oneself like a covered object, it needs activity to recover. For example, a mirror gives clear reflection when it is cleaned or rubbed which otherwise is an activity.

(6) Another remark made by the opponent of Vedānta is that though the self is different from body, it is identified with body, hence disembodiedness comes after the fall of the body or after death.

Śaṅkarācārya has answered all the possible doubts and questions that were usually raised by the opponents of Vedānta in his times.

Scriptures are essential

Śaṅkarācārya says that all the Upaniṣadic sentences assert and reveal the nature of *Brahman*. *Brahman* is the perceivér, creator and sustainer of everything. He was there before the creation of the universe. On the basis of the statement *tat tvam asi* ('that thou art'), *Brahman* is spoken as the self within us. It does not mean that we know *Brahman* with some means, but it is said that except through the scriptures *Brahman* cannot be known through any standard of knowledge (*pramāṇa*). To perceive *Brahman* and self as separate entities is ignorance, it is duality (*dvaita*). When *Brahman* is perceived as self and the unity is achieved, duality will cease, and liberation, which is the highest aim of man, will be attained.

Śaṅkarācārya rejects the opponent's view that the Upaniṣads are useless as they speak of an existing thing. Śaṅkara replies that the Upaniṣads import the knowledge of *Brahman* to remove the veil of ignorance. For example, in darkness whenever one perceives a rope as a snake, then he gets fear. To remove this fear caused by the misapprehension, one has to be advised: This is not a snake, it is a rope. In the similar way the Upaniṣads speak of *Brahman* to remove the cognition that projects the self as transmigrating.[15] In actuality the self is transcendental.

Brahman-knowledge and mokṣa

According to Śaṅkarācārya meditation is prescribed for the purification and concentration of mind. It is a subsidiary factor, in the context of people who believe that *Brahman* has name and form, for attaining liberation by gradual stages. He says that meditation is not exclusively enjoined for attaining *Brahman*, but it is a secondary means apart from the study of the Vedānta texts. Śaṅkara points out that the section dealing with religious rites and duties, and the sections concerned for *Brahman*-knowledge are different from each other, their results are heaven (*svarga*) and liberation (*mokṣa*) respectively.[16]

In this connection Śaṅkarācārya writes about the gradations of happiness: Happiness is the result of virtue while sorrow is for vice. Similarly after death, performers of rites and sacrifices travel through the way of the gods (*deva-yāna*); whereas the followers of virtues like austerity, truthfulness, hospitality, clarity, *ahiṁsā* (non-violence) travel through the way of the fathers (*pitṛ-yāna*). Those who go by the way of the fathers will come back, after reaching the world of moon, to this world in order to experience the residual *karma*. So, the present birth of certain people with all happiness and sorrow is the result of their past life and actions. Thus in the world there are different gradations of happiness and sorrow for beings and human beings in accordance with their actions in the past life.[17]

In contrast to the above gradations of happiness, the knower of *Brahman*-knowledge is untouched by happiness and sorrow. The knower of *Brahman* attains liberation (*mokṣa*). *Mokṣa* is the state of bodilessness, which is eternal. It is beyond past, present and future. It is neither related to the results of actions

15. Swamī Gambhīrānanda, *op. cit.*, p. 25.
16. *Ibid.*, p. 24.
17. *Ibid.*, p. 27.

nor to results of good deeds; it comes after the attainment of the knowledge of *Brahman*. The Upaniṣads say that he who knows *Brahman* becomes *Brahman*.[18] For example, the seer Vāmadeva realised that he was *Brahman*, and he has neither performed sacrifices nor served the gods. This is being established in the great sentence (*mahāvākya*): *aham brahmāsmi* (I am *Brahman*). As such the Upaniṣads assert that the *Brahman* is the inner self of the seeker or knower. After the realisation of the Self, the difference between the known, the knower, and the knowledge vanishes.[19] The *Bṛhadāraṇyaka* Upaniṣad says that one cannot see that which is the witness of vision, and one cannot know that which is the knower of knowledge. In other words, there will not be any difference between knower and known. It is cessation of duality. It is neither a product by mental and physical activity nor modification or transformations of something like curd. *Mokṣa* is not something to be attained from outside, for it is the intrinsic nature of one's own self. *Mokṣa* does not need any action for its manifestation like after cleaning a mirror the object reflects brightly and clearly.[20]

In this context, Śaṅkarācārya rejects ritual-bathing, wearing sacrificial thread and, etc., as they are intended only to purify the body but not the self. He says that whatever take place within the body will effect what is related to it; the pure self which does not related to the body needs no purification. For example, if a man thinks that he is sick he takes some medicine and becomes healthy. Similarly, whosoever thinks himself impure takes a bath; and whosoever considers himself with the body performs all kinds of actions (*karma*s). *Mokṣa* has nothing to do with the body; and it is not to be achieved through purification, but it is the state of one's identity with *Brahman*.[21]

Again referring to the opponents' view that even acquiring knowledge is a kind of mental action. Śaṅkarācārya says that

18. Swamī Gambhīrānanda, *op. cit.*, p. 28.
19. *Ibid.*, p. 31
20. *Ibid.*, p. 33.
21. *Ibid.*, pp. 32, 34.

performances of actions depend upon man's will; meditation can be done or not done, it depends up man. Contrary the knowledge of *Brahman* differs from mental action, it is apprehension of things as they are; hence knowledge is not something to be done or not done. Therefore, he says that though knowledge is a mental action, it has a great difference, and cannot be considered as action.[22] In this connection Śaṅkara gives an example: Thinking of a woman as fire is a *karma* in Vedic rituals but in our ordinary experience we cannot consider a woman as fire. But since the scriptures enjoin us to consider woman as fire, we take it for granted. On the other hand, realisation of the self as *Brahman* is not a mental action, but an apprehension.

Seeker of Brahman

Śaṅkarācārya points out that even Yājñavalkya's advise to his wife Maitreyī should not be considered as a sort of injunction. In this dialogue meditation was asserted for the seeker of *Brahman*-knowledge to continue his search for *mokṣa* to avoid the seeker falling in the worldly affairs. It is meant for the seeker to keep away from the affairs of the world. Śaṅkara says that if one realises his self as *Brahman* he discontinues the performance of actions for worldly benefits.[23] Realisation of the unity of the self is not an act but apprehension of the self as *Brahman*. That is why no injunction is enjoined for the realisation of *Brahman*. Because the self cannot be denied as it is the very self of one who denies it. The self is the witness of the idea that denies the existence of the self. The self, that experiences the idea of 'I', exists in all creatures. It is all-pervasive consciousness, without any difference of degrees. The *karma-kāṇḍa* portion of the Vedas and the logicians do not know it. Any one cannot deny the self, because the denial itself is the manifestation of the self. It is beyond rejection and acceptance. It is all-pervasive entity, the *puruṣa*. *Puruṣa* is changeless, eternal, intelligent and free. The

---

22. Swamī Gambhīrānanda, *op. cit.*, p. 34.
23. *Ibid.*, p. 36.

Upaniṣads speak of *puruṣa*. Thus the self is known from the Upanisads.[24]

What is the use of instruction about the unknown thing? It is another question of the opponent. Śaṅkarācārya says that the knowledge imparted about the unknown things helps to eradicate the ignorance, which causes this worldly state. He says that the life of the man who has realised the unity of the self and *Brahman* cannot be proved that his way of life continuous just as before when he identifies himself with body, but this identification ceases when the identification with *Brahman* is achieved. For example, a rich man worries of his wealth for fear of theft. However if he becomes a monk, he will not be miserable for any loss of the wealth. Similarly, one may be proud of having an earring, but he will not be unhappy if he lost it after he becomes a monk. This is what the *vedāntin* calls disembodiedness.

The idea of embodiedness comes when body and self are identified. It is the result of false-ignorance.[25] The self is not related to body. Due to non-discrimination the self is identified with body. The identification of the self with body is not a figurative expression as stated in the example, 'He is a lion'. In this example a man is compared to a lion, because he has the qualities of a lion such as bravery and cruelty. Self and body identification is due to ignorance. In the darkness one may take for granted the stump of a tree for man and nacre for silver. Even the wise people do not make distinction in using words like the shepherds and goatherds. Thus since embodiedness is the result of false-ignorance, it is said that the knower of *Brahman* has no embodiedness even while living. The knower of *Brahman* in this world lives like a dead snake in the midst of ants.[26] The *Bhagavad Gītā* says that he is in *samādhi*, in him there is total absence of any impulsion to work. In this connection, Śaṅkarācārya says:

24. Swamī Gambhīrānanda, *op. cit.*, p. 37.
25. *Ibid*. p. 40.
26. *Ibid*., p. 42.

> Hence a man who has realised his own identity with *Brahman* cannot continue to have the worldly state just as before, whereas the man continues to have the worldly state just as before has not realised his identity with *Brahman*.[27]

To sum up Śaṅkarācārya says that *śravaṇa*, *manana*, *nididhyāsana* are meant for giving rise to knowledge and they are not separate entities. The study of the Upaniṣadic texts reveals that *Brahman* is known from scriptures. If *Brahman* is known only through *upāsanā* (wishful meditation) there is no need to write the *Brahma Sūtra*, because Jaimini has written aphorisms by starting with the aphorism: *athāto dharma-jijñāsā*. The Jaimini aphorisms are written to help the performance of sacrifices and to attain human objectives. They do not deal with *Brahman*-knowledge, accordingly Bādarāyaṇa has undertaken the writing of the *Brahma Sūtra* to assert the knowledge of the unity of the self and *Brahman*.

---

27. Swamī Gambhīrānanda, *op. cit.*, p. 43.

10

Minor Works and Hymns of Śaṅkarācārya

THE greatest research work on Advaita Vedānta is Paul Deussen's *The System of Vedānta*. In this work Deussen brought out the fundamentals of Advaita Vedānta on the basis of Śaṅkarācārya's commentary on the *Brahma Sūtra* of Bādarāyaṇa. This monumental work has been the source of inspiration for understanding Śaṅkarācārya's theology, psychology and cosmology by the later writers on Vedānta. But in recent times the accessibility of the commentaries of Śaṅkara on the Upaniṣads and the *Bhagavad Gītā* have made the academicians and followers of Vedānta to have more comprehensive understanding of the teachings of Śaṅkara. Not only the triple-texts (*prasthānatrayī*) but also the books attributed to Śaṅkara, especially the minor works (*prakaraṇa grantha*s) and hymns (*stotra*s) have helped to bring out various facets of Śaṅkara's thought.

Apart from the commentaries, it is believed that Śaṅkarācārya has written many treatises like the *Viveka cūḍāmaṇi* and the *Upadeśa-sahasrī*. These works are called the *prakaraṇa grantha*s which etymologically means 'Chapter like Books' or pamphlets or 'Positive cause Books'. The *prakaraṇa grantha*s were written in verse and prose form varying from a single *śloka* to a thousand *śloka*s. They contain the main teachings of Śaṅkara as well as certain impressive clarifications about the relationship between the student and the teacher.

In Advaitic tradition we come across how the disciples have

carried out and interpreted the sayings of their teachers especially the hymns. A hymn reflects adoration towards a deity. A study and description of the minor works and hymns of Śaṅkarācārya help us to understand more about Śaṅkara's position and theology. Scholars like T.M.P. Mahadevan and Duncan Greenless have analysed the various hymns of Śaṅkara. An attempt to provide a brief introduction to every available work in this respect has been made here irrespective of the authenticity of the work ascribed to Śaṅkara.

Viveka-cūḍāmaṇi

The *Viveka-cūḍāmaṇi*, which contains 581 *śloka*s (stanzas), stands first in the Advaitic tradition for the propagation of the theology of Śaṅkarācārya through a form of teacher-student (*guru-śiṣya*) relationship. The *Vivekacūḍāmaṇi* was translated by Mohini M. Chatterji and has been published by the Theosophical Society in 1932. Subsequently, Swāmī Mādhavānanda of Advaita Ashram, Calcutta, has translated it in 1966. But with a more substantial commentary by Śrī Jagadguru Candraśekhara Bhāratī, this work has been translated by P. Śaṅkaranārāyaṇa with a good intro duction and analytical content.[1] Mohini M. Chatterji's translation of the *Viveka-cūḍāmaṇi* is brief and very easy to understand.[2]

Viveka-cūḍāmaṇi means 'crest-jewel of wisdom'. It is a theological treatise and explains the fundamentals of Advaita Vedānta. The subject-matter is presented in a dialogue form between a teacher and a student. The Introduction deals as to how to attain *mokṣa* through discrimination between eternal and non-eternal. Śaṅkaranārāyaṇa in this context remarks as follows:

> *Viveka-cūḍāmaṇi* is a philosophical treatise expounding the cardinal truths of Advaita Vedānta, according to which, liberation or *mokṣa* can be acquired only by *jñāna*.[3]

---

1. *Vide* P. Śaṅkaranārāyaṇa, tr., *Viveka-cūḍāmaṇi*, 1973.
2. *Vide* Mohini M. Chatterji, tr., *Viveka-cūḍāmaṇi*, 1983.
3. P. Śaṅkaranārāyaṇa, *op. cit.*, p. vi.

The *Viveka-cūḍāmaṇi* is a popular book among the sages of Advaita tradition, especially the Swāmīs of Sarada Peetham, Śṛṅgerī. This work lays down remarkable prerequisites to know the knowledge of *Brahman* on the part of the disciple and teacher. The disciple should possess *jijñāsā* (desire), *adhikāra* (competence), *vinaya* (discipline) and *vairāgya* (unattachment); on the other hand, the teacher must be a *sadguru* (perfect teacher) and bestow *anurāga* (compassion) upon the disciple. In other words, a disciple should be an individual possessing humility apart from the four prerequisites of knowledge (*sādhana catuṣṭaya*); and the teacher must be a man of essential knowledge, compassion and truthfulness.[4]

The main theme of the *Viveka-cūḍāmaṇi* is to describe the inner self of man as the cosmic self. After a fruitful discussion the disciple experiences the ecstasy of attaining the state of the highest knowledge by realising his non-difference from the *paramātman* (Supreme Self). This is an elevation of the individual self from the empirical world to that of the transcendental level by the divine experience of *Brahman*, *brahmānubhava*.[5]

Though *nirguṇa* Brahma is the ultimate truth, *Viveka-cūḍāmaṇi* describes *saguṇa* Brahma also. This implies that at the *vyāvahārika satya* (empirical level) the role of the *saguṇa* Brahma cannot be denied. In this context, the *Viveka-cūḍāmaṇi* does not mention any essential forms of the worship of a personal God. *Bhakti* (devotion) has been entertained in the thirty-second *śloka* of *Viveka-cūḍāmaṇi* as the factor along with others to attain liberation:

> *mokṣa kāraṇa samāgrayam bhakti revā garīyasī* ।
> *svasvarūpānusandhānam bhaktirityābhiyate* ।।

> Among the set of means to bring out *mokṣa*, *bhakti* (devotion) is the greatest. Continuous contemplation of one's essential nature (*svarūpa*) is said to be the *bhakti*.[6]

4. P. Śaṅkaranārāyaṇa *op. cit.*, p. vii.
5. *Ibid.*, p. xvii.
6. *Viveka-cūḍāmaṇi*, 32. Cf., P. Śaṅkaranārāyaṇa, *op. cit.*, p. 48.

Here the teachers of Vedānta interpreted *anusandhāna* (meditation) as *nididhyāsana*; and devotion is a part of it. However, the commentator remarks that devotion alone cannot lead the seeker to *mokṣa*. As devotion is a result of the sense of difference and delusion, therefore others upheld this viewpoint. It is doubtful how the opponent's view is brought out here in a dialogue between a teacher and a disciple because *Viveka-cūḍāmaṇi* is not a commentary but an exposition. It may be said that after possessing the four prerequisites along with *śravaṇa*, *manana* and *nididhyāsana*, the *Brahman*-seeker is advised to go to a truthful and qualified teacher to obtain the instruction and also *bhakti* as an additional qualification. Whatever the interpretations may be, the *Viveka-cūḍāmaṇi* contains the cardinal truths of Advaita Vedānta in simple terms without ambiguous disputations.

The *Viveka-cūḍāmaṇi* asserts the need of a teacher (*guru*) for attaining knowledge, it uses mostly the Upaniṣadic words and verses. The entire Vedāntic message has been set forth in a compact form for clear understanding. The *Viveka-cūḍāmaṇi* can be compared to the *Bhagavad Gītā* for Advaita Vedānta as the later stands for Indian theology. Each verse of the *Viveka-cūḍāmaṇi* is a proverb, a quotation and a great sentence revealing the truths of Vedānta for guiding people. It is a book of norms, ethics, principles, suggestions and practices.

> *vedānthārtha vicāraṇa jāyate jñānamuttamam* ।
>
> Perfect knowledge arises from understanding Vedānta-meaning.[7]

To sum up, the *Viveka-cūḍāmaṇi* clearly records

- The need of a teacher for attaining the highest knowledge.
- Actions (*karmas*) do not lead one to liberation.
- Prerequisites for *Brahman*-knowledge.
- Renunciation of *ahaṁkāra* (egoism).

7. *Viveka-cūḍāmaṇi,* 47. Cf., Mohini M. Chatterji, *op. cit.*, p. 23. It is a free translation.

- The three *guṇa*s and state of the Self.
- A discussion about *sūkṣma śarīra* and *liṅga śarīra*.
- Five sheaths of the self.
- The doctrine of *Brahman*.
- Concepts like *nirvikalpa-samādhi*, *savikalpa-samādhi*, *vikṣepa-śakti* and *avarṇa-śakti* (which makes one thing as another).
- the characteristics of *jīvanmukta*
- Description of *prārabdha*, *sañcita* and *āgāmī karma*s.

The greatest message of *Vivekacūḍāmaṇi* is that 'bondage and liberation are indeed false' and 'are created by *māyā* (illusion)'[8] and it proclaims:

na nirodha, naco utpatti na bandho naco sādhakaha ।
na mumukṣu navai mukti itseya paramārthatā ।।

There is neither restraint, nor birth, nor bondage, nor an adept (to aid the disciple), nor one desirous of liberation, nor one liberated this is the highest truth.[9]

Upadeśa-sahasrī

The *Upadeśa-sahasrī* (A Thousand Teachings) written by Śaṅkarācārya contains prose and poetry parts and has been translated into English with explanatory note by Swāmī Jagadānanda in 1941.[10] The *Upadeśa-sahasrī* is a teacher's manual to enlighten the student about the distinction between self and one's body, mind, etc., in order to make him to comprehend the unlimited bliss of the Lord.[11]

---

8. *Viveka-cūḍāmaṇi*, 572, cf. Mohini M. Chatterji, *op. cit.*, p. 210.
9. *Viveka-cūḍāmaṇi*, 575, *ibid.*, p. 211.
10. Swāmī Jagadānanda, tr., *Upadeśa-sahasrī: A thousand teachings*, 1979.
11. *Ibid.*, Preface, p. iii.

The prose part of *Upadeśa-sahasrī* is divided into three chapters, comprising 116 verses. The first chapter contains the way in which the disciple is to be enlightened. The four prerequisites discussed in the *Brahma-Sūtra-Bhāṣya* are analysed, and *Brahman* as the Supreme Being is clearly described with many words and terms and also defined as the all comprehensive principle. *Brahman* is explained as the innermost self; and the name and form are said to be temporal, and the knowledge of Śruti and Smṛti destroys ignorance by establishing the one-self of all.[12]

The second chapter, like the first chapter, is a discussion between teacher and student, who has approached a teacher being vexed with the transmigratory nature of the self. The teacher explains to him the knowledge of the Supreme Self. The problem of the superimposition of the substratum on the thing or self is explained and the states of the self are discussed.[13] The third chapter deals with the method of realisation of the knowledge of *Brahman* on the part of a man who hankers after liberation.[14]

The metrical part of the *Upadeśa-sahasrī* is divided into 19 chapters with 1000 *śloka*s. In the beginning the role of the Upaniṣads to enlighten the individual to come out of the bondage of birth and death is explained. It is said that the self is pure consciousness and identical with *Brahman*. *Brahman* is described as that which is without attributes, and discrimination helps the individual to know that the individual self is not different from the Supreme Self. It is stated that a man who gets liberation will be without fear, desires and grief.[15] *Brahman* is pure consciousness, and one experiences the Self in dreamless sleep. It is said that one who attains *Brahman*-knowledge is free from family life (*saṁsāra*) and without delusion. The *Brahman*-knower

---

12. *Upadeśa-sahasrī: A thousand teachings*, p. 27.
13. *Ibid.*, p. 36.
14. *Ibid.*, p. 71.
15. *Ibid.*, p. 89.

does not feel that he belongs to such and such caste and such and such state. *Brahman* is without attributes and the *Brahman*-knower is always free from mental modifications and delusions. *Brahman*-knower becomes *Brahman*; considers himself changeless, free, pure, awaken and without qualities.[16]

The author of the *Upadeśa-sahasrī* writes that the wise man should give up his caste, etc.,[17] and should be free from all ideas of 'me' and 'mine'[18] to attain *Brahman*. The relation of body and its connection with attributes — senses, pleasures and five elements are explained; and the wise men are advised to be free from them. Right knowledge is said to be the supreme purifier and the greatest secret of Vedānta saves one from the great ocean of births and deaths.[19]

The eighteenth chapter of the *Upadeśa-sahasrī* is the biggest chapter being called as the *tat tvam asi prakaraṇam* describing the fundamentals of Advaita Vedānta by criticising the opponent's views.[20] In this chapter the great sentences (*mahāvākya*s) *tat tvam asi* and *aham brahmāsmi* are described and popular examples like 'rope-snake' and 'not this, not this' are given.[21] Thus the *Upadeśa-sahasrī* is a compendium of the teachings of the Advaita Vedānta meant for people who live in religious monasteries (*guru-kula*s) to be taught by teacher to their disciples. It is primarily a metaphysical discourse aiming to make the disciples to know the knowledge of *Brahman*. In the end of the text it is said that the *Upadeśa-sahasrī* contains the substance of the Upaniṣads and written by the great teacher Śaṅkarācārya, the *paramahaṁsa parivrājaka*.

Ātma-bodha

Ātma-bodha means 'the teaching of the self' or 'teaching to the

16. *Upadeśa-sahasrī: A thousand teachings*, p. 134.
17. *Ibid.*, p. 153.
18. *Ibid.*, p. 166.
19. *Ibid.*, p. 217.
20. *Ibid.*, pp. 219, 285.
21. *Ibid.*, pp. 219, 224.

self', but translators have used to mean it self-knowledge or knowledge of the self. Swāmī Nikhilānanda of the Ramakrishna-Vivekananda Centre of New York has translated *Ātma-bodha* into English and it was published in 1947 with a good introduction containing the essence of Śaṅkarācārya Vedānta.[22] Another translation by S.S. Cohen was also available being published in 1975.[23] Swāmī Nikhilānanda says that *Ātma-bodha* inculcates perennial interest and universal value. He writes:

> Self-knowledge is vital. All other forms of knowledge are of secondary importance.[24]

The *Ātma-bodha* 'the teaching about the self' according to the interpretation by Nikhilānanda is certainly deals with the individual self. But if an individual considers his self as physical creature, he will be selfish and tries to accumulate everything for himself and remains a selfish-man which otherwise leads to difference, destruction and fight. On the other hand, if one regards his self as the self of all with a spiritual bent of mind he follows the path of unselfishness. Thus, spiritualisation of the self leads to 'peace and happiness of all'.[25]

The text of the *Ātma-bodha* contains 68 *śloka*s (verses) intended to provide *mokṣa* for those who have ceased from sins and craving through practising peace and penance. The essence of Advaita Vedānta, the unity of *ātman* and *Brahman* has been explained throughout the stanzas with the popular concepts used in Advaita messages and interpretations of the commentaries of Śaṅkarācārya on the *prasthānatrayī*. The *Ātma-bodha* instructs in brief the truths of Advaita Vedānta as follows:

- 'Liberation cannot be attained without knowledge' — verse, 2
- 'Action cannot destroy ignorance' — verse 3

22. Swāmī Nikhilānanda, *Self-knowledge*, 1978, pp. 149-31.
23. S.S. Cohen, *Advaitic Sādhanā or the Yoga of Direct Liberation*, 1975, pp. 55-88.
24. Swāmī Nikhilānanda, *op. cit.*, pp. xx-xxi.
25. *Ibid.*, Preface, p. xxi.

- 'The family life is like a dream filled with attachment and aversion, etc.' — verse, 6
- 'The world appears to be real, but it seems to be silver in a nacre' — verse, 7
- 'In waking state (conduct) attachment and aversion, pleasure and pain, and mind are real, but in deep-sleep-state nothing exist, thus they do not belong to self (*ātman*)' — verse 22.
- 'The body is perishable like bubbles' — verse, 30.[26]

The *Ātma-bodha* asserts the attributelessness of the Self in eight characters:[27]

1. *nirguṇe* (attributeless)
2. *niṣkriye* (actionless)
3. *nitye* (eternal)
4. *nirvikalpe* (destructiveless)
5. *nirvikāre* (deformless)
6. *nirākāre* (formless)
7. *nitya muktosmi* (ever liberated)
8. *nirmala* (calm, pure)

Again the *Ātma-bodha* records a number of Upaniṣadic sentences and examples found in Śaṅkarācārya's commentaries like:

- Illusion of snake for a rope (*rajju sarpa vāda*),
- The supreme *Brahman* is truth, knowledge and infinite (*satyam jñānam anantam yat param brahma meva tat*).[28]
- A liberated soul while living, a living-free is the nature of existence, knowledge and bliss (*satcidānanda rūpatvāt jīvanmukta*).[29]

---

26. Swāmī Nikhilānanda, *op. cit.*, pp. 152-3, 159-60, 182, 192.
27. *Ibid.*, p. 195.
28. *Ibid.*, pp. 188, 196.
29. *Ibid.*, p. 209.

Thus *Ātma-bodha* concludes:

> *Brahman* is other than the universe.
> Apart from *Brahman* nothing exists.
> Should anything appear to exist, it is as unreal as a mirage (*marumarīcaka*).

All that is seen or heard is not other than *Brahman*. Through knowledge of the reality (*tattva jñāna*) the universe appears to be the 'non-dual *Brahman*, which is existence, consciousness and Bliss (*satcidānanda madvayam*)'.[30] Following remarks by S.S. Cohen further asserts the greatness of *Ātma-bodha*, he states:

> *Ātma-bodha* is one of the smallest treatises written by Ācārya Śaṅkara, but it occupies a unique place in the science of self-knowledge of liberation. . . . In 68 short stanzas the celebrated author gives the cream of the Vedānta.[31]

Dakṣiṇa-mūrti-stotra

The *Dakṣiṇa-mūrti-stotra* is a hymn of Śaṅkarācārya addressed to the south facing God, *dakṣiṇa-mūrti*. Alladi Mahādeva Śāstrī translated it into English in 1899, which also contains Sureśvarācārya's exposition and commentary called *Mānasollāsa* or the brilliant play of thought. Apart from these texts the *Praṇava-vārttikā* of Sureśvarācārya and another Upaniṣad called *Dakṣiṇa-mūrti Upaniṣad* are included and translated by Alladi Mahādeva Śāstrī.[32] This work contains a descriptive introduction by Mahādeva Śāstrī about the various systems of Vedic religion while expounding the main principles of the system of Vedānta. An attempt has been made to show the difference between Vedānta and other Schools. He remarks that the four great sentences of the Upaniṣads are expounded to establish the unity of *ātman* and *Brahman*.[33]

---

30. Swāmī Nikhilānanda, *op. cit.*, pp. 223, 225.
31. S.S. Cohen, *op. cit.*, p. 53.
32. Allādi Mahādeva Śāstrī, tr., *Dakṣiṇa-mūrti-stotra*, 1978.
33. *Ibid.*, p. xi.

1. Intelligence is *Brahman* — *Aitareya Upaniṣad.*
2. I am *Brahman* — *Bṛhadāraṇyaka Upaniṣad.*
3. That Thou Art — *Chāndogya Upaniṣad.*
4. This Self is *Brahman* — *Māṇḍūkya Upaniṣad.*

The *Dakṣiṇa-mūrti-stotra* contains ten hymns addressed to Lord Śiva by whose grace according to the author one realises the teachings of Advaita. It is explained that there should not be any distinction between the teacher and the taught, as per the spirit of Advaita (non-duality). The teacher is referred to God whereas the taught to self. T.M.P. Mahadevan translated the hymn into English and was published in 1970.[34] In total, it contains 10 poems and each poem at the end is suffixed with the word *dakṣiṇa-mūrti*. The *Dakṣiṇa-mūrti* is the Lord Śiva who is represented as a world teacher with his youthful face teaching the disciples about the unity of the individual self and Supreme Self. Following is the substance of the each hymn:

1. To *Dakṣiṇa-mūrti*, the *māyā* is like a dream and He sees the Universe as a city reflected in the mirror, when He rises in the morning, He Himself a teacher.

2. *Dakṣiṇa-mūrti* is a great sage and through His will, He created the Universe of name and form.

3. The world seems to be different from Supreme Self but not so, He gives *mokṣa* for those who realise that what is there in the world is there in the individual self; *tat tvam asi*.

4. The knowledge of the Supreme Self pass through every individual and universe like the light-rays of a lamp when covered by a pot with many holes.

5. People, who consider the body, senses and ego as the self are blind, deluded in *māyā*; those who come out of this illusion attain *mokṣa*.

6. One who comes out breaking the power of *māyā* and by

34. T.M.P. Mahadevan, *The Hymns of Śaṅkara*, 1980, pp. 1-26.

withdrawing sense-organs will be like a sun or moon after eclipse.

7. The Lord with his blessed hand appears to the disciples as their own self in all states.
8. People who are deluded by *māyā* see the universe with its difference like a man who dreams in sleeping and waking states.
9. The Supreme Lord encompasses the Universe and is all-pervading, nothing exists out of Him.
10. By hearing, reflecting and meditating, the Supreme Self can be realised as the self in all.

The essence of the *Dakṣiṇa-mūrti-stotra* is to inculcate in man a devotion to the Lord by keeping in mind the percepts of the great *māhā-vākya*s of the Upaniṣads like *tat tvam asi*. Therefore, it may be pointed out that *Dakṣiṇa-mūrti-stotra* does not differ from the main teachings of Vedānta; but extols a belief, a faith and devotion with reference to the oneness of *ātman* and *Brahman*.

Śivānanda-laharī

The *Śivānanda-laharī* is another hymn ascribed to Śaṅkarācārya by tradition. It was translated into English by T.M.P. Mahadevan.[35] It contains 100 *śloka*s of four lines each. The central theme of the *Śivānanda-laharī* is devotion to God, Śiva who is the giver of happiness and provider too. The hymns have been written in a beautiful form and content in a double meaning (*śleṣa*) expressing the feelings of the Lord to his maiden. On the other hand, the relationship between God and a devotee is expressed with deep devotion. The *Śivānanda-laharī* as a hymn to Śiva stressed the greatness of Śiva by using stories and legends found in the Purāṇic literature. Śiva is projected as the Supreme God, the saviour of souls and giver of good things.[36]

---

35. *The Hymns of Śaṅkara*, pp. 78-171.
36. *Ibid.*, p. 79.

Bhakti described by Śaṅkarācārya in this hymn is specific with an emphasis on spiritual discipline. It involves the orientation of mind in its thinking, feeling and willingness towards God constantly making the mind to get absorbed itself in God.[37] All categories of the mind such as *citta*, *buddhi*, *manas*, *dr̥ṣṭi* and *hr̥daya* which are considered as reflective organs of the mind are to be diverted towards God as their goal. The devotee has to concentrate his mind on God alone; this is compared to the longing of the swan for the tank, *cakravāka* bird for the sun, *cātaka* bird for the rain cloud.[38] Like that the relationship of man and God is expressed with the worldly examples; and the mind has been described as an elephant that roams in all directions in the forest and Śiva is described as the Lord who binds the mind and creates *bhakti* (devotion). A hymn in the *Śivānanda-laharī* runs as follows:

> O Destroyer of the cities! Do bind the elephant
> of my heart to the peg of the feet with
> the chain of devotion, dragging it speedily with
> the help of the God of courage and the machinery
> of intelligence, so that it may not stray.[39]

It is said that the mind and heart should be offered to God; the Lord is the saviour and protector, and king of kings. The mind is said to be a maiden fit to serve the Lord. A woman by circumstances away from home always thinks of her husband like that mind always should think of the Supreme Lord and dissolve itself in the contemplation of God.[40]

T.M.P. Mahadevan, the greatest authority on Advaita Vedānta says that in the *Śivānanda-laharī*, Śaṅkarācārya had adopted the devotional path of Śaivites for *Brahman*-realisation. Devotion to God, meditation upon Śiva is also an Advaitic experience. By quoting a number of verses from the *Śivānanda-*

37. *The Hymns of Śaṅkara*, p. 79.
38. *Ibid.*, p. 80.
39. *Ibid.*, p. 168.
40. *Ibid.*, p. 81.

laharī T.M.P. Mahadevan has explained devotion as a means to attain the knowledge of the non-difference of *ātman* and *Brahman*, which is liberation.

Bhaja-Govindam

The *Bhaja-Govindam* is a hymn in praise of Govinda, the Lord God. T.M.P. Mahadevan translated it in 1962 and included in his book.[41] He says that the *Bhaja-Govindam* was composed by Śaṅkarācārya to inculcate worship and adoration towards God in the minds of scholars, and it contains 31 hymns of four lines each.

All the 31 verses of the *Bhaja-Govindam* start with the word *bhaja-govindam*. The main theme of thẹ hymn is to teach the disciples the true knowledge of *Brahman*, which gives liberation. In the *Bhaja-Govindam* the disciples are classified into two kinds: pure and impure. It is said that there is no use in disputation, therefore disputes among the followers of different scholars are to be avoided or discouraged. Advaita Vedānta asserts non-duality and the teaching of *Bhaja-Govindam* makes one to become perfect and ultimately leads him to *mokṣa*. The *Bhaja-Govindam* is a work intended to the disciples to instruct them in the funda mentals of Vedānta.

Actually, *Bhaja-Govindam* means worship-service of Govinda, the name for Lord Kr̥ṣṇa. However, Śaṅkarācārya interprets Govinda as the highest reality. In this connection, T.M.P. Mahadevan has given the various meanings and modes of worship of the word *bhaja*, they are as follows:

1. Listening of the glory of God (*śravaṇa*)
2. Singing the praise of God (*kīrtana*)
3. Thinking of God (*smaraṇa*)
4. Adoration of the feet of God (*pāda-sevana*)
5. Offering worship to God (*arcana*)
6. Making obedience to God (*vandana*)

---

41. *The Hymns of Śaṅkara*, pp. 33-7.

7. Servitude to God (*dāsya*)
8. Friendship with God (*sakhya*) and
9. Self-gift to God (*ātma nivedana*).[42]

42. *The Hymns of Śaṅkara*, p. 40.

11
Teachings of Śaṅkarācārya

THE philosophy of Śaṅkarācārya has been summarised in three verses:

> *Brahman* is real (*Brahma satyam*)
> The Universe is Unknowable (*jagat mithyā*)
> *Brahman* and *ātman* are not different (*jivo brahmaiva na paraḥ*).[1]

The later thinkers formed this maxim to show the spirit of Advaita Vedānta. It is highly impossible for everybody to study the interpretations given by Śaṅkarācārya as his literary activity was enormous. This chapter exclusively narrates the spirit of Śaṅkarācārya's doctrines based upon his commentaries on the *prasthānatrayī*.[2]

Scripture, perception and inference

Though the tradition of Advaita Vedānta accepts six *pramāṇa*s (standards of knowledge) as explained in the Vedānta *parībhāṣā*, Śaṅkarācārya has referred to the scripture (*śāstra*), perception (*pratyakṣa*) and inference (*anumāna*) only. But the later writers have included the other standards, namely comparison (*upamāna*), postulation (*arthāpatti*) and non-cognition

---

1. *Brahma-jñānāvalīmālā*, 5.21., Cf., Swāmī Prabhavānanda, *The Spiritual Heritage of India*, 1977, p. 283.
2. The Doctrines have been summarised based on the selections found in T.M.P. Mahadevan, *Śaṅkarācārya*, 1968.

(*anupalabdhi*).[3] All these six standards were actually formulated by the Mīmāṁsā School of Kumārila Bhaṭṭa. Again to remark, the treatment of perception, inference and scripture by Vedānta School is the same as that of Nyāya School. With reference to the other three standards, namely comparison, postulation and non-cognition, the views of Nyāya School are somewhat different. Therefore, it is appropriate to deal with what Śaṅkarācārya actually discussed in his interpretations of the *prasthānatrayī*. Apart from the *śāstra* (scripture), Śaṅkarācārya mentioned *pratyakṣa* and *anumāna*.

Śaṅkarācārya asserts that scripture (*śāstra*) is the only source of knowledge to decide what is good and what is bad. Consequently, he is of the opinion that an individual cannot rely upon himself for the knowledge of good and bad. According to the *Bhagavad Gītā Bhāṣya*, the Upaniṣads, Itihāsa-Purāṇas and Smṛtis are considered to be the scriptures (*śāstra*s); and the Upaniṣads come under Śruti. In the *Brahma-Sūtra-Bhāṣya* it is mentioned that if there is a conflict between Śruti and Smṛti or among Smṛtis regarding some point of view, the Śruti or the Smṛti which agrees with the Upaniṣads should be accepted. Śaṅkarācārya is aware of the limits of scripture (*śāstra*). He says that scripture (*śāstra*) is not authoritative in connection with things of immediate experience. He remarks that if the Śruti says that fire is cold, one should not believe it or take it for granted.

Śaṅkarācārya points out that *Brahman* cannot be known from mere argumentation. He criticises the self-styled wise men (the logicians) who admit the difference between oneself and the other. The logicians for him are first rate heretics and liars.

According to Śaṅkarācārya the role of a teacher (*ācārya*) in acquiring knowledge and for enlightenment is very much important and necessary. In many texts he asserts that knowledge generated by the scriptures (*śāstra*s) and teacher

---

3. For a detailed understanding of these *pramāṇa*s see: R. Puligandla, *Fundamentals of Indian Philosophy*, 1985, pp. 208-11.

helps one to attain the knowledge of *Brahman*. Even the well-versed in scriptures (*śāstras*) should not seek for the knowledge of *Brahman* independently, but should approach a teacher who is blessed with self-control, control of body and inner sense and also kind enough. The teacher must have respect for the Vedic transmission through the line of a teacher and students.

Śaṅkarācārya states that the knowledge of *Brahman* derives from the Upaniṣads. By considering the Upaniṣads, Itihāsa-Purāṇas and Smṛtis as scriptures (*śāstras*) he says that they are valid means for the knowledge of *Brahman*. They are not only final authority on *Brahman*-knowledge but also on what ought to be done and what ought not to be done. The knowledge of good and bad derives from scriptures only. They point out what is right and what is wrong, but do not force any one to follow either of the ways. People have to choose the means according to their tastes. Scriptures help those who are in the state of bondage or ignorance.[4]

Śaṅkarācārya says that the Vedas have an independent authority. They do not derive their authority from any other source and independent of any other means of knowledge. The aim of them is to direct the people in relation to their goals, especially they connected with religious rites. The Vedas are not the prerequisites to learn the *Brahman*-knowledge. The study of the Upaniṣads is enough to discuss the knowledge of *Brahman*.[5] Śaṅkarācārya quoted many times the sayings of the Upaniṣads as Śruti passages in his commentaries. The scriptures are valid means to know things beyond sense perception, but not authority in connection with the things of immediate experience. Through the harmonisation of the Vedāntic sentences, the knowledge of *Brahman* is possible.

---

4. Śaṅkarācārya's views on the conception of *jñāna* (knowledge) and *śāstras* (scriptures) have been extensively discussed in P. George Victor, *Social Philosophy of Vedānta*, 1991 pp. 137-46.
5. *Brahma-Sūtra-Bhāṣya*, 2.1.1; *Bṛhadāraṇyaka Upaniṣad Bhāṣya*, 2.3.6; 2.4.10, *Taittirīya Upaniṣad Bhāṣya*, 1.11.4; *Brahma Sūtra Bhāṣya*, 1.1.1. Cf. P. George Victor, *op. cit.*, p. 143.

> In the inquiry into *dharma* (religious duty), scripture, etc., alone are authoritative; not thus in the case of the inquiry into *Brahman*. But, scripture, etc., and experience, etc., are authorities here, as they become possible; for, *Brahman*-Knowledge has experience as its culmination, and has the existent reality as its content.[6]

The sentences of the Vedas and Upaniṣads are valid with reference to their respective spheres only. He also says at different passages that the sentences uttered by teachers or the advice of a teacher also help one to attain the knowledge. A sentence becomes valid when a trustworthy person or a teacher utters it. To that extent the Vedāntic tradition emphasises *śravaṇa*, *manana* and *nididhyāsana*. Yājñavalkya has stated this to his wife Maitreyī in the *Bṛhadāraṇyaka Upaniṣad:*

> Loo, Verily, it is the Soul (*ātmā*) that should be seen, that should be hearkened, that should be thought on, that should be pondered on, O Maitreyī.[7]

Thus Śaṅkarācārya respects scriptures (*śāstras*) as valid means of knowledge.

Perception (*pratyakṣa*) is the comprehension of the sensible objects through the specific mental states of the individual. It is the direct consciousness of objects obtained through the exercise of the senses. According to Advaita Vedānta, in any state of the individual, perception of a thing is same as long as that state remains unchanged. Our perception of certain things is real with reference to the principles of that state only; and whenever the state is disturbed the perception of the thing will also be disturbed and changed. For example, the experiences of the dream-state are real with reference to the principles of that dream state only. And it is a fact that we know the dreaming experiences are

---

6. *Brahma-Sūtra-Bhāṣya,* 1.1.2., Cf., T.M.P. Mahadevan, *Śaṅkarācārya*, 1969, pp. 79-80.
7. *Bṛhadāraṇyaka Upaniṣad*, 2.4.5. Cf., R.E. Hume, *The Thirteen Principal Upaniṣads*, 1949, p. 100.

false when we come into the waking state. The conclusion is that all our knowledge of the objects of the external world is real until the absolute knowledge attained. Śaṅkarācārya says that the knowledge comes through perception is real with reference to the empirical world only. He says that if the scripture says that fire is cold, one should not believe it or take for granted.[8] On the other hand, perception is useless in the matters of transcendental experience. Śaṅkarācārya says that the 'knowledge of *Brahman* is outside the range of perception':

> . . . for *Brahman*'s relation with anything cannot be grasped. It being outside the range of sense-perception. The senses naturally comprehend objects, and not *Brahman*.[9]

Inference (*anumāna*), according to Advaita Vedānta, is based upon specific past impressions, and co-ordinates our notions of two things. It is made by our notion of concomitance (*vyāpti-jñāna*) between two things. Generally, inference may be described as the process of reasoning which enables us to conclude certain happenings, which are not perceived on the basis of the past experience or observations. Vedānta does not establish formal validity of the inference. On the other hand, when it is not contradictory to the scriptures, Vedānta accepts inference related to the knowledge that presented previously. Inference is a method of agreement upon two things through past impressions. For example, when smoke comes out of the windows of a kitchen, we believe that there is a fire in the kitchen. Accordingly when there is smoke on a hill, we infer that there is fire on the hill. Thus smoke serves as a mark of fire. Advaita Vedānta maintains that all appearances are unbelievable as in the case of perceiving a conch-shell as silver. Hence Śaṅkarācārya maintains that all things in the world are indefinable (*anirvacanīya*).

---

8. *Bhagavad Gītā Bhāṣya*, 18:66.
9. *Brahma-Sūtra-Bhāṣya*, 1.1.2.

Brahman-ātman

The fundamental teaching of Advaita Vedānta is the identity of *Brahman* and *ātman*. *Brahman* is the eternal principles of all beings in the universe. *Brahman* is the power, which creates sustains and absorbs itself into all beings and the universe. It is within us, and is identical with *ātma*. This self (*ātma*) of each one of us is not a part but wholly and absolutely the eternal, indivisible *Brahman*. Thus ourselves are of *Brahman*, and this is expressed in the words: *tat tvam asi* ('that art thou') and *aham brahmāsmi* ('I am *Brahman*'). S. Radhakrishnan, the greatest commentator on Indian philosophy precisely says:

> The aim of the Vedānta is to lead us from an analysis of the human self to the reality of the one absolute self. . . . This system is the *vijñānātman*, which is subject to changes while the *paramātma* is free from all change. The *jīva* is said to be in essence one with the *ātma*. That art thou.[10]

Though the individual self is the Supreme Self (*Brahman*), due to *avidyā* (ignorance) the self identifies itself with body. It is the empirical standpoint, from which the self is connected with the limiting adjuncts (*upādhis*) such as body and senses. These limiting adjuncts make the self to believe that it is the enjoyer and agent (*bhoktā* and *kartā*) of the bodily actions. The fruits of the actions done in a birth are to be reaped either in that birth or the subsequent birth. Thus actions and their results and the prescribed recompensatory actions form a chain without an end, and attached to the beginningless and endless *saṁsāra*. *Saṁsāra* (family life) is the state of pain and pleasure of the body in this world. Actions and their results are connected with the body but not the self. But *saṁsāra* is due to identification of the limiting adjuncts and body with the self. The cessation of *saṁsāra* is possible when right knowledge of the Self attained. Right-

10. Radhakrishnan, *Indian Philosophy*, vol. II, 1940, p. 595.

knowledge consists of positive and negative aspects to perceive body and self as separate entities and to perceive the Supreme Self (*Brahman*) as the self (*ātman*) within us. When the identification of *Brahman* and *ātman* is achieved duality will cease, and liberation is possible.

Śaṅkarācārya says that the *ātman* is not different from *Brahman*, because nothing exists apart from *Brahman*. *Brahman* is the cause for the origin, sustenance and dissolution of all beings and things in the world and the universe itself. The self cannot be regarded as a little part of *Brahman*, because *Brahman* is changeless and without parts. *Brahman* comprehends all beings in Him, and each of us is nothing but the changeless and indivisible *Brahman*. *Brahman* as the inner self (*ātman*) of us is neither enjoyer nor agent of actions performed by the body. On the other hand, it is the witness (*sākṣin*) of the actions and experiences of the body.

Brahman and Īśvara

In Vedānta passages *Brahman* is spoken without attributes as the Absolute and again described with attributes. To reconcile these two views, Śaṅkarācārya postulated two standpoints: *pāramārthika-satya* and *vyvāhārika-satya*. At the level of *pāramārthika-satya* (highest truth) *Brahman* is non-dual and without plurality, and the self is nothing but *Brahman*. At the level of *vyāvahārika-satya* (empirical truth) which is relative, *Brahman* is conceived to be the cause of the world and with attributes. Thus the later conception forms the popular religion for all those who cannot raise themselves to the level of *pāramārthika-satya*. Consistent with his two levels of truth, Śaṅkarācārya admitted two conceptions of *Brahman* (Supreme Self/Absolute God):

1. *Brahman* or *nirguṇa* Brahma (Supreme God without qualities).
2. *Saguṇa* Brahma or *Īśvara* (God with good qualities).

Śaṅkarācārya says that *Brahman* is without any qualities

or attributes (*guṇas*), differences, forms and limiting adjuncts. It is the inexpressible, invisible, unaudible and unthinkable ground of all existence. The *Bṛhadāraṇyaka Upaniṣad* says that *Brahman* is not to be heard of and not to be felt and not to be perceived. It is different from what we know and what we do not know. The *Taittirīya Upaniṣad* states that words and thoughts do not fit to describe *Brahman*. The only assertion that can be made of *Brahman* is that it is 'not this, not this' (*neti*, *neti*).

> That Soul (*ātmā*) is not this, it is not that (*neti*, *neti*). It is unseizable, for it cannot be seized, indestructible, for it cannot be destroyed; unattached, for it does not attach itself; is unbound, does not tremble, is not injured.[11]

The Upaniṣads say that *Brahman* is the real (*sat*), inner self of all and witness everything. Thus, it is said as pure intelligence (*cit*). The *Taittirīya Upaniṣad* maintains that *Brahman* is pure bliss (*ānanda*). Accordingly, in the later writings, *Brahman* is described as *sat-cit-ānanda* (pure being, pure intelligence and pure bliss).[12] This conception of *Brahman* is *nirguṇa*, according to Śaṅkarācārya. It is neither the cause, nor the creator, nor the sustainer, nor the destroyer of the universe. *nirguṇa* Brahmā is pure reality beyond name and form. It cannot be worshipped. This conception of *nirguṇa* Brahmā relates to the highest standpoint of reality or truth.

At the lower empirical truth (*vyāvahārika-satya*), *Brahman* is considered with qualities. Śaṅkarācārya says for the purpose of worship and for the sake of ignorant people, *Brahman* is spoken in the scriptures with qualities, differences, forms and limiting adjuncts. Owing to these limiting adjuncts *Brahman* is referred

---

11. *Bṛhadāraṇyaka Upaniṣad*, 4.5.15. Cf. R.E. Hume, *op. cit.*, p. 147.
12. In the verse 49 of *Ātma-bodha* a minor work attributed to Śaṅkara it is said that *jīvanmukta* endowed with Self-knowledge realises the existence, knowledge and bliss of *Brahman*. Again the concept was found in 56, 64 verses of *Ātma-bodha*. Paul Deussen states that this conception was not found in the commentaries of Śaṅkara but occurs in *Nṛsiṁhatāpanīya Upaniṣad*. *Vide* his, *The System of Vedānta*, 1972, p. 212.

to as the personal God or *Īśvara*. This conception of *Brahman* is lower, conventional, relative and related to practical standpoint. *saguṇa* Brahma is the personal God who stands in relation to man and the world. It is *saguṇa* Brahma that man worships in different names and forms. The *Chāndogya Upaniṣad* describes *Brahman* as all working, all-wishing, all-tasting, all-smelling and all-embracing. The *Muṇḍaka Upaniṣad* mentions that the sun and the moon are the eyes, the wind his breath and the cardinal points are ears. *Saguṇa* Brahma is the God, thought of as the cause, creator, sustainer and destroyer of the Universe. In this way *Brahman* is described as omnipotent, omniscient and omnipresent. Śaṅkarācārya comments that *saguṇa* Brahma is spoken for those who worship and expect happiness, but not knowledge and *mokṣa*. The result of worship is similar to that of actions (*karmas*); so the worshipper of *saguṇa* Brahma (*Īśvara)* attains happiness and after death reaches heaven through the way of the gods (*deva-yāna*).

Śaṅkarācārya recognised the need for the conception of *saguṇa* Brahmā to generate religious consciousness in ignorant men. It helps to cultivate moral virtues necessary for the realisation of *nirguṇa* Brahma. *Saguṇa* Brahma serves as the stepping stone for one to lead for knowledge of Reality, Supreme Self, and Absolute *Brahman*. However, Śaṅkara stresses that knowledge of *Brahman* can be attained, if one transcends the conception of *saguṇa* Brahma. But one has to remember that the knowledge of *nirguṇa* Brahma alone is the knowledge of Reality; and *mokṣa* is possible through it only.

Māyā and world

The conception of *māyā* has a significant place in Vedāntic view. In the *Ṛgveda* the word *māyā* occurs many times to indicate the supernatural powers attributed to various gods such as Varuṇa, Mitra and Indra. It is used as a world sustaining power and as deceptive and cunning nature of the *asuras* (devils).[13] The word

---

13. Cf., from Jaikishandas Sadani, 'Concept of Māyā in Vedānta' in Prabhakara Machive, ed., *Bharatiya Samskrit*, vol. I, 1983, pp. 344-63.

māyā appears in the *Bṛhadāraṇyaka Upaniṣad* as a quotation from the *Ṛgveda*, wherein it is stated that Indra has assumed various forms through his *māyā* (supernatural power) and created all the beings. The *Praśna Upaniṣad* maintains that to attain *Brahman* world, one should not possess trickery (*māyā*). Again the *Śvetāśvatara Upaniṣad* outlines that through His *māyā*, Brahmā projected this world; He creates *māyā* and the world is *māyā*. After the cessation from *māyā* the attainment of *Brahman* is possible. This idea of cosmic-illusion is the basis for the doctrine of *māyā* in the Upaniṣads and writings of later Vedānta.

Śaṅkarācārya says that *Brahman* alone is real and the world is unreal, and *Brahman* is the cause for the origin, sustenance and dissolution of the world. How does Śaṅkarācārya justify the relation between the real *Brahman* and the unreal world — is a doubt for opponents of Vedānta. But Śaṅkara says that the relation between *Brahman* and the world is indefinable, *anirvacanīya*. He says that the world resides in *Brahman* like the illusion of a snake in the rope. *Māyā* is our persistent tendency which regard appearance as reality. It is our ignorance *avidyā* that can not distinguish difference between appearance and reality. In other words, ignorance is the foundation of *māyā*. According to Śaṅkara, *māyā* is beginningless, endless, unthinkable and inexpressible.

Advaita Vedānta maintains that *Brahman* is the only Reality, hence it is said that *māyā* is the power that conceals the absolute *Brahman* under name and form. Therefore, *Brahman* becomes *Īśvara* with reference to empirical standpoint. *Māyā* has the power of concealing things, it projects the unreal as real and vice versa. Since *māyā* is thus deceptive in character, it is called *avidyā* (ignorance) or false-knowledge. Śaṅkarācārya and other Advaita *vedāntin*s speak of *māyā* and *avidyā* interchangeably. *Avidyā* is regarded as prior to *māyā*, because *māyā* presupposes *avidyā* (ignorance). This also means that *māyā* disappear when *avidyā* is destroyed by the knowledge of *Brahman*. For example, the snake imagined in a rope is not something that exists, hence it can be removed by discrimination. Śaṅkara points out that the magic-show produced by a magician is not something real, but being ignorant of the magician's trick we mistake appearance for reality. However, for the magician, who is the master of the trick there is no *māyā*. When we discover the magician's trick, we will be no longer the victims of the trick or illusion. Similarly, due to *māyā* the world of diversity, variety and multiplicity is considered real; when the knowledge of *Brahman* or the real knowledge is attained, one is no longer held captive by *māyā* (unknowableness).

The Vedānta passages assert that *Brahman* alone is real and unchanging, while the world of multiplicity, plurality, name and form is changing. *Brahman* is the underlying power and ground of all existence and the world. The world of our senses and intellect is merely a world of names and forms having no reality apart from *Brahman*, just as different objects made of clay are not permanent but only the substance, clay is real and permanent.

Similar to the Upaniṣadic explanation, Śaṅkarācārya says that the whole world has emerged from *ākāśa* or ether. First of all, from *Brahman* the *ākāśa* or ether arises, from which air, fire, water and earth followed subsequently. Śaṅkarācārya has not explained a systematic account of creation; and asserts that the relation between *Brahman* and the world is indefinable, *anirvacanīya*. He says that the world has no existence apart from *Brahman*. Śaṅkarācārya supported the Gauḍapāda's theory of creation, according to which the world is not evolved or produced, but seems to be so, on account of limited insight. Śaṅkarācārya did not accept the view of *pariṇāma-vāda* or the theory of transformation. According to him, the world is not a part that transformed from *Brahman*, as *Brahman* is devoid of parts. To illustrate the difficulty of the world problem, Śaṅkarācārya employed certain analogies. He says that *Brahman* appears as the world like the rope appears as the snake. While understanding *māyā* and *avidyā* in Vedānta literature we have to keep the following two things in mind:

1. *māyā* (unknowableness) is related to the world.
2. *avidyā* (ignorance) is associated with individual.

According to Śaṅkarācārya, the world of phenomena with plurality, name and form is the product of ignorance (*avidyā*). The external world, phenomenal world is unknowable, hence concluded as illusion (*māyā*). The whole world is an illusion and will continue throughout one's own life unless man becomes aware of the truth by perfect knowledge. It is just as the illusion of a snake in rope, or the illusion of a man while walking in a dark night, where there is only a tree trunk, or the illusion of water in a mirage which one can refute by closer observation. A magician creates magic, throws a rope into the sky and climbs it; and the magician is unaffected by the magic. Similarly, *Brahman* projects this world and is unaffected by it. The world of appearance is the realm of illusion, depends on ignorance. It is like the figures in dreams, in which figures and experiences are true as long as one remains in dreaming state; and when one awakes from the dreaming state the figures and experiences of the dreaming state will disappear. When one frees himself from ignorance, the world of appearances itself will be seen as *Brahman*. In other words, the world of plurality, name and form is neither different from *Brahman*, nor *Brahman* itself, it is *anirvacanīya* (indescribable).

> For this reason also, the things perceived in waking are illusory; they do not exist at the beginning or in the end. That, which does not exist at the beginning or in the end, e.g., mirage, etc., does not exist in the middle also: this is the settled view in the world. So, these things that are perceived in waking are illusory.[14]

Jñāna-mārga and karma-mārga (Path of knowledge and path of action)

Śaṅkarācārya did not criticise the rituals in view of his assertion of the path of knowledge (*jñāna-mārga*). His family is associated with the tradition of Vedic beliefs and rites. The interpretation of rituals as the lower form of worship does not mean that the rituals are denied; on the other hand, it is clearly stated that the

---

14. T.M.P. Mahadevan, *Śaṅkarācārya*, 1968, p. 96.

path of action (*karma-mārga*) is related to the ignorant and the path of knowledge (*jñāna-mārga*) for the wise. The *jñāna-mārga* with its emphasis on learning *Brahman*-knowledge and by following renunciation (*saṁnyāsa*) is the highest path, while the *karma-mārga* is a round-about method. As said earlier, at the lower level of one's being the *karma-mārga* is acceptable. The aim of Śaṅkarācārya is not to deny the fact of life but to argue that among these two paths, the *jñāna-mārga* is superior when compared to the *karma-mārga*. As per the grades among men the paths are also fixed. As most people are limited to mundane actions and it is impossible for them to come out of the lower level, therefore the lower modes of worship are appropriately given so that they can progress themselves to the higher level. In this connection, T.M.P. Mahadevan records a verse as follows:

> The first stage is Image worship; the next consists in *japa* and prayer; still higher is mental worship; the highest is of the form 'I am He'.[15]

It does not mean that Advaita Vedānta is theistic but it prefers the higher level and go beyond theism. The Absolute *Brahman* is really unconditioned and beyond personification. However, as the object of adoration for man and in order to serve as the ground of the Universe, the Absolute is interpreted as of personal. It should not be understood that *Brahman* is degraded to *Īśvara*, on the contrary it is *Īśvara* that should be realised, in subsequent experience, as *Brahman*.

As long as man is in the state of waking, he experiences the external world of things. Among the three states, waking state is unique, in the sense that it is the only state where man experiences that he has to live in this world, being bound by ignorance and strive for *mokṣa*. Thus instead of seeking the infinite end, man pursues the finite ends — wealth and pleasure. If man sought these ends within the laws of *dharma*, the door to the way for the commencement of the spiritual journey will be opened. Anything that comes through actions is bound to perish,

---

15. *Śaṅkarācārya*, p. 65.

on the other hand, knowledge releases one from all the fetters of life. The ignorance of man can be removed by the knowledge of *Brahman*. The point to remember here is that, there is no doubt that the path of knowledge (*jñāna-mārga*) is the right path for realisation, but it is also a fact that the path of action (*karma-mārga*) plays its role in the lower level (*vyāvahārika-satya*). Śaṅkarācārya did not want to rebuke the injunctions of the Vedas.

The path of knowledge (*jñāna-mārga*) consists of listening (*śravaṇa*), reflection (*manana*), and meditation (*nididhyāsana*) activities on the part of *Brahman*-seeker. At the same time performance of one's duties without attachment to results is also intended to produce certain qualifications that make one eligible for the path of knowledge.[16] Accordingly the four pre-requisites are mentioned in the *Brahma-Sūtra-Bhāṣya*. The Vedas lay down the rituals, provide prayers and hymns for those who have relatively dull intellect in order to guide them away from sensual pleasures, desires and lust. This kind of knowledge is considered as lower knowledge. The higher knowledge, which the Upaniṣadic portions speak of consists intellectual study and experiencing *Brahman* (*brahmānubhava*). It is the highest conception of *Brahman* without qualities. The finite mind of man cannot conceive the infinite *Brahman*. As long as man lives in the world, he uses any tool, which comes to his hand for his own *mokṣa*. Therefore, the lower state of knowledge is neither to be despised nor regarded as a concession to the ignorant man. In support of this argument, the author of a very popular book on Śaṅkarācārya remarks as follows:

> The personal God (*Īśvara*) gradually brings the individual man to realise that the individual self and *Īśvara* and the limitless *Brahman* are in essence the same thing.[17]

Śaṅkarācārya being the product of Vedic tradition would not despise the Vedic commandments. As long as the lower level of reality (*vyāvahārika-satya*) is concerned the rituals are as much necessary as the study of Upaniṣads in the higher level

16. *Śaṅkarācārya*, p. 70.
17. Y. Keshava Menon, *The Mind of Ādi Śaṅkara*, 1976, pp. 13-14.

(*pāramārthika-satya*). When Śaṅkara says that the scriptures or the Vedas are eternal and infallible, he means that the rituals are intend for the lower state and the study of Upaniṣads for the higher state. Thus the contradiction between the Vedas and Upaniṣads is resolved; and man has to find his place to fit himself in order to choose his path.

Vyāvahārika-satya and pāramārthika-satya (Phenomenal truth and noumenal truth)

We should not forget the synthesis made by Śaṅkarācārya by keeping balance between the two kinds of truths:

1. The Relative or Phenomenal truth (*vyāvahārika-satya*) of lower level.
2. The Absolute or Noumenal truth (*pāramārthika-satya*) of higher level.

According to Śaṅkarācārya at the lower level, man acts and perceives through senses and reasoning with a state of superimposition; he believes in the world of appearance and dwell in the realm of *māyā*. On the other hand, at the higher level man is beyond the subjective and objective difference and transcends the lower knowledge and comprehends the highest *Brahman*. Śaṅkara clearly maintains that the lower knowledge is valid in the world of appearance. It means that rituals are applicable until man realises the higher knowledge and comprehends the highest *Brahman*. This should not be considered that Śaṅkara is combining the path of knowledge and the path of action. He maintains the relevance of the two paths in their own orbits but opposes the combination of them. In accordance with this spirit Chandradhara Sharma writes that *karma* and *upāsanā* are subsidiary to knowledge:

> A liberated sage, however, performs actions without any attachment and works for the upliftment of humanity. Sankaracharya's own life bears ample witness to this fact.[18]

18. Chandradhara Sharma, *A Critical Survey of Indian Philosophy*, 1976, p. 286.

Mokṣa

The highest goal of man, according to Śaṅkarācārya, is *mokṣa* (liberation). It is the state of absolute freedom from ignorance (*avidyā*), unknowableness (*māyā*) and family life of suffering (*saṁsāra*). It is the state beyond the cycle of birth and death. Simply speaking, *mokṣa* is nothing but realisation of the individual self as *Brahman*. According to Advaita Vedānta, *mokṣa* is not something to be achieved, but it is the very nature of the self. It is not something that follows after death, and it is not to be understood in the sense of endless existence in some distant and unknown world. It is the attainment of the highest state of consciousness through identifying the self (*ātma*) as *Brahman*. It is to be attained here and now while one is still in ones bodily existence. In other words, it is the realisation of non-difference of the individual self from the absolute Self. *Mokṣa* is called 'experiencing non-duality' (*advaita-anubhava*). A man who attains such consciousness is called 'the living-free', *jīvanmukta*.[19]

Śaṅkarācārya says that except the knowledge of *Brahman*, discussed in the Vedānta texts, there is no other means for *mokṣa*. *Mokṣa* is disembodiedness from ignorance; embo diedness is due to the ignorance of identifying the self with the body, etc. It is recorded in the *Bṛhadāraṇyaka Upaniṣad Bhāṣya* and *Bhagavad Gītā Bhāṣya* that the seeker of *mokṣa* has to renounce all actions. One must be free from all attachments, passion for women and external things. In the *Brahma-Sūtra-Bhāṣya*, Śaṅkarācārya points out four pre-requisites (*sādhana catuṣṭaya*) for the seeker of *Brahman*-knowledge, which leads to *mokṣa*. They are:

1. Discrimination between the eternal and the non-eternal.
2. Dispassion for the enjoyment of the fruits of actions either here or in the other world.
3. Possession of control of mind and senses, turning away from things of senses, and developing forbearance, concentration and faith.

---

19. R. Puligandla, *op. cit.*, p. 227.

4. Desire for liberation

He says that if these are present, one may desire to know *Brahman*. According to Śaṅkarācārya, knowledge means knowledge of the Self, which is acquired from the Upaniṣads and a teacher. The study of Vedānta texts involves *śravaṇa*, *manana* and *nididhyāsana* (hearing, reflection and meditation). *Śravaṇa* is listening to the sages as they expound the great truths of the Upaniṣads and study of the Vedānta texts. *Manana* is the stage of reflection to understand the meaning of the Upaniṣads through systematic analysis and investigation to strengthen the truths of the Upaniṣads. *Nididhyāsana* is the process of concentration to realise the truth as the only one Reality. Through profound meditation only one becomes and experiences that he is indeed *Brahman*, the true Reality. A man who thinks that he is different from *Brahman* performs actions and sacrifices. When one realises that the very self (*ātman*) is the Supreme Self (*Brahman*), he no longer performs action. Then one overcomes the duality and ignorance, and attains liberation. The *Brahman*-knower becomes *Brahman*.

12

Methodology of Śaṅkarācārya

THE *20th Century Chambers Dictionary* defines 'methodology' as a set of rules and proceedings in doing things in a defined way.[1] When Śaṅkarācārya's life, mission and teachings are studied and perceived, one can understand that he has a methodology.

Scripture as standard (śāstra as pramāṇa)

As early as in February 1959 Prof. K. Satchidananda Murty in his Ph.D. thesis, *Revelation and Reason in Advaita Vedānta*,[2] has exclusively discussed for the first time the epistemology of Advaita Vedānta. A parallel work of this nature, similarly a Ph.D. thesis by Prof. N.K. Devaraja came out in publication in 1962.[3] Both these scholars have dealt with the epistemology of Śaṅkarācārya. In the following pages Śaṅkara's epistemology has been undertaken in view of his methodology.

Epistemology is the study of source, nature and limitations of valid knowledge. When we refer to the histories of Indian philosophy with reference to the Vedānta School of Śaṅkarācārya, S.N. Dasgupta maintains that comparison (*upamāna*), presumption (*arthāpatti*), testimony (*śabda*) and non-congition

---

1. E.M. Kirk Patrick, ed., *Chambers 20th Century Dictionary*, 1985, p. 791.
2. K. Satchidananda Murty, *Revelation and Reason in Advaita Vedānta*, 1974.
3. N.K. Devaraja, *An Introduction to Śaṅkara's Theory of Knowledge*, 1972.

(*anupalabdhi*) of this School are similar to the views of Mīmāṁsā School and treats perception (*pratyakṣa*) and inference (*anumāna*) separately.[4] R. Puligandla asserts that

> the Advaita Vedanta treatment of perception (*pratyaksha*), inference (*anumana*) and testimony (*sabda*) is essentially the same as that of the Nyaya School.[5]

The most authoritative writer on Advaita Vedānta, Paul Deussen, on the basis of *Brahma-Sūtra-Bhāṣya* states:

> As far as our *Vedānta sūtra*s are concerned, there is, neither in the text nor in the commentary, any discussion of the *pramāṇa*s at all.[6]

However, in Vedānta tradition, he says that Bādarāyaṇa considers Śruti, i.e., the Upaniṣads and Smṛti, i.e., the *Bhagavad Gītā*, *Manu Dharmaśāstra* and other books as the sources or standards of knowledge. Bādarāyaṇa rejected perception and inference as separate standards of knowledge. In the *Bṛhadāraṇyaka Upaniṣad Bhāṣya*, while denying action as means for liberation, Śaṅkarā cārya states the five standards, viz., perception, inference, comparison, presumption and scriptural testimony.[7] In this connection he says that any function of action (*karma*) has no support from any one of these standards. As such, he says that action (*karma*) can produce or bring or modify or purify something only. If we examine it, the validity of these standards are considered to qualify the role of action (*karma*) or valid with reference to action (*karma*) but not in the case of *Brahman*-knowledge.

Śaṅkarācārya asserts that scripture (*śāstra*) is the only source of knowledge to decide what is good and what is bad.[8]

---

4. S.N. Dasgupta, *A History of Indian Philosophy*, vol. I, 1975, p. 471.
5. R. Puligandla, *op. cit.*, p. 208.
6. Paul Deussen, *op. cit.*, 1975, p. 89.
7. *Bṛhadāraṇyaka Upaniṣad Bhāṣya*, 3.3.1 (introduction). Cf. Swāmī Mādhavānanda, tr., *The Bṛhadāraṇyaka Upaniṣad with the Commentary of Śaṅkarācārya*, 1965, p. 449.
8. *Brahma-Sūtra-Bhāṣya*, 3.1.25.

Consequently, he is of the opinion that an individual cannot rely upon himself for the knowledge of good and bad. Scriptures (*śāstras*) are not only authority for what ought to be done and what ought not to be done, but also they are final authority, and valid means of the knowledge of *Brahman*.[9] According to the *Bhagavad Gītā Bhāṣya*, the Upaniṣads, Itihāsa-Purāṇas and Smṛtis are considered to be the scriptures (*śāstras*); and the Upaniṣads come under Śruti.[10] In the *Brahma-Sūtra-Bhāṣya* it is mentioned that if there is a conflict between Śruti and Smṛti or among Smṛtis regarding some point of view, the Śruti or the Smṛti which agrees with the Upaniṣads should be accepted.[11] Śaṅkarācārya is aware of the limits of scripture (*śāstra*). He says that scripture (*śāstra*) is not authoritative in connection with things of immediate experience. He remarks that if the Śruti says that fire is cold, one should not believe it or take it for granted.[12]

Śaṅkarācārya points out that *Brahman* cannot be known from mere argumentation. He criticises the self-styled wise men (the logicians) who admit the difference between oneself and the other. The logicians for him are 'first rate heretics and liars'.[13]

According to Śaṅkarācārya, the role of a teacher (*ācārya*) in acquiring knowledge and for enlightenment is very much important and necessary. In many texts, he asserts that knowledge generated by the scriptures (*śāstras*) and a teacher helps one to attain the knowledge of *Brahman*.[14] Even the well-versed in scriptures (*śāstras*) should not seek for the knowledge of *Brahman* independently, but should approach a teacher who is blessed with self-control, control of body and inner sense and kind enough. The teacher must have respect for the Vedic

---

9. *Bṛhadāraṇyaka Upaniṣad Bhāṣya*, 2.11.
10. *Bhagavad Gītā Bhāṣya* 18.66; Introduction to third chapter.
11. *Brahma-Sūtra-Bhāṣya* 2.1.1.
12. *Bhagavad Gītā Bhāṣya*, 2.1.20.
13. *Bṛhadāraṇyaka Upaniṣad Bhāṣya*, 2.1.20.
14. *Bhagavad Gītā Bhāṣya*, 3.41; 18. 16, 55, *Bṛhadāraṇyaka Upaniṣad Bhāṣya*, 2.1.20; 2.5.15; *Praśna Upaniṣad Bhāṣya* 6.5.

transmission through the line of a teacher and students.[15] Thus Śaṅkarācārya respects scriptures (*śāstra*s) as valid means of knowledge.

Writing commentaries

To propagate the ideals of Vedānta, Śaṅkarācārya has written a number of commentaries on *Īśa, Kena, Kaṭha*, *Praśna*, *Muṇḍaka*, *Māṇḍūkya*, *Aitareya*, *Taittirīya*, *Chāndogya*, *Bṛhadāraṇyaka* Upaniṣads and also on the *Bhagavad Gītā* and the *Brahma Sūtra*. The remarkable achievement and commitment of Śaṅkarācārya is evolving himself into a commentator (*bhāṣyakāra*).

Śaṅkarācārya's commentary reflects a number of verses from the Vedic literature and the later works. The nature of Śaṅkarācārya's explanation and procedure is like that of the Saint Paul's letters, wherein references are found from early books of the *Bible* to the *Gospels* on Christ. Further we find arguments in support of his thesis and critical retrospection of certain Vedic commandments. He raises the possible doubts and questions and thereby answers them. Professor Hiltrud Rustau aptly says:

> Śaṅkarācārya, in its full extent, has used the philo sophical knowledge of his time, and he himself enriched the philosophical discussion very much by arguing comprehensively with all the important systems of that time.[16]

The procedure of Śaṅkarācārya involves two objectives: (a) harmonisation of the Upaniṣadic sentences, and (b) explanation of the meaning of the words and phrases. For example, the harmonisation of different accounts of the definition of *Brahman* have fell upon Śaṅkara and the result was the two conceptions

---

15. *Muṇḍaka Upaniṣad Bhāṣya*, 1.2.12; *Brahma-Sūtra-Bhāṣya*, 1.3.28.
16. Hiltrud Rustau, 'The Place of Sankara in Indian Philosophy and His influence on Modern Indian Thinkers', in R. Balasubrahmanian and Sibajivan Bhattacharya, ed., *Perspectives of Sankara*, 1989, p. 382.

of the same Reality, the *saguṇa* Brahmā and *nirguṇa* Brahmā. Apart from harmonisation, he took the job of explaining the meaning of words. For example, the 555 aphorisms (*sūtras*) of Bādarāyaṇa are unintelligible without commentary. But Śaṅkara has interpreted them all and undertaken the great-sentences (*mahāvākyas*), while commenting the Upaniṣads; they include:

1. I am *Brahman* (*aham brahmāsmi*)
— *Bṛhadāraṇyaka Upaniṣad*, 1.4.10.

2. That art thou (*tat tvam asi*)
— *Chāndogya Upaniṣad*, 6.8.7.

3. *Brahman* is wisdom (*pra-jñānam brahma*)
— *Aitareya Upaniṣad*, 3.5.3.

4. This self is *Brahman* (*ayam ātma brahma*)
— *Bṛhadāraṇyaka Upaniṣad*, 2.5.19.

In the *Brahma-Sūtra-Bhāṣya* Śaṅkarācārya has supported his stand and writes 'here is commenced an assertion of the meaning of the texts of Upaniṣads'.[17]

Missionary travels

Śaṅkarācārya believes that discussions and conferences will help to understand the scriptures. While commenting upon the instruction of Yājñavalkya to king Janaka, he points out that conferences are sought to decide subtle religious matters and they will help to understand different capacities of a number of scholars.[18] The episode of Śaṅkarācārya's debate with Maṇḍana Miśra and his wife, and the establishment of the monasteries in the four centres of India — Śṛṅgerī in Mysore, Dvārakā in Gujarat, Purī in Orissa and Badrīnāth in Uttarāñcala, shows his missionary zeal. In his lifetime, though short lived, he had attracted some disciples who became famous such as Sureśvara (who was formerly Maṇḍana Miśra, according to some sources), Padmapāda, Ṭoṭaka and Hastāmalaka.

17. *Brahma-Sūtra-Bhāṣya* 1.1.1.
18. *Bṛhadāraṇyaka Upaniṣad Bhāṣya*, 3.2.15.

Rejection of opponent views

In the *Brahma-Sūtra-Bhāṣya*, Śaṅkarācārya says that in course of establishing the right meaning of the Upaniṣads and, etc., the rejection of opponent's view is necessary.[19] To this extent, he remarks that one has to refute the different views of logicians, which are based upon garbled quotations and sophistry.[20] Śaṅkara explains in the *Brahma-Sūtra-Bhāṣya* that there were conflicting doctrines of Lokāyatas and Buddhists in practice; so to refute their doctrines he has to give the right meaning of the Vedānta sentences. According to him, people are in need of a direction to get emancipation. Therefore, Śaṅkara took the job of interpretation and the negation of the opponents' views.

The dualist

Śaṅkarācārya perceives the Vedic literature in two different parts and thereby explains their applicability to the mankind. Though he was a non-dualist, his approach with reference to his analysis is dual: Ignorant and wise, *karma* and *jñāna*, *saguṇa* Brahmā and *nirguṇa* Brahmā, *deva-yāna* and *pitr̥-yāna*. The following table shows his analysis and perception:

	Lower	**Higher**
The Vedas	*karma-kāṇḍa*	*jñāna-kāṇḍa*
*Vidyā*s	*apara-vidyā*	*para-vidyā*
Human beings	Ignorant	Wise
Paths (*mārga*)	*karma*	*Jñāna*
Transmigration	*pitr̥-yāna*	*deva-yāna*
Wisdom	*pravr̥tti*	*nivr̥tti*
Reality (*satya*)	*vyāvahārika*	*pāramārthika*
Brahma	*saguṇa*	*nirguṇa*

In the *Brahma-Sūtra-Bhāṣya*, Śaṅkarācārya distinguishes the two kinds of knowledge:

1. *para vidyā* (higher knowledge), the knowledge of *Brahman*.

19. *Brahma-Sūtra-Bhāṣya*, 2.2.1.
20. *Ibid.*, 1.1.5.

2. *apara vidyā* (lower knowledge), the knowledge of actions.

According to him *śikṣā*, *niruktam*, *kalpa*, *vyākaraṇam*, *chandas* and *jyotiṣam* as well as the *Ṛgveda* are considered to be lower knowledge, while the knowledge of the Upaniṣads is higher. Accordingly the Upaniṣads come under *jñāna-kāṇḍa* portion and the Vedas come under *karma-kāṇḍa* portion. Śaṅkarācārya distinguishes two conceptions of *Brahman*; *Brahman* with qualities and *Brahman* without qualities, respectively known as *saguṇa* and *nirguṇa*. Men are considered into two groups: the wise and the ignorant. As long as ignorance continues in man there is a need for the performance of actions (*karmas*) and rituals. In the introduction to the third chapter of the *Bhagavad Gītā Bhāṣya*, Śaṅkarācārya points out that wisdom consists of two aspects: the path of actions (*pravṛtti*) and the path of renunciation (*nivṛtti*). He says that *jñāna* and *karma* are opposed to each other like light and darkness, and their results are different. When ignorance is burnt away by the knowledge, liberation is possible. From this standpoint the ignorant who perform actions follow the way of fathers (*pitṛ-yāna*) and those who worship *Brahman* but regard *Brahman* different from themselves enter the way of gods (*deva-yāna)* after death. It is interesting that the non-dualist Śaṅkarācārya has adopted the dualistic method to uphold his non-dualism (Advaita).

Parables

Śaṅkarācārya believes that the stories taught in the Upaniṣads are meant to teach certain values of life. He gives certain stories (*upamānas*) in his commentaries. Śaṅkarācārya says that in the *Bṛhadāraṇyaka Upaniṣad*, the story of Gārgya and Ajātaśatru is meant to teach the rules of conduct and also it suggests that faith is an important factor to learn *Brahman*-knowledge, and warns about mere argumentation.[21] He says that the separate existence of the individual self arises from the delusion generated by limiting adjuncts (*upādhis*) — the body, senses, etc. In relation to this a parable mentioned by Śaṅkara is as follows: A certain

---

21. *Bṛhadāraṇyaka Upaniṣad Bhāṣya*, 2.1.1.

prince was discarded by his parents and was brought up by a fowler. The prince, who was unaware of his princely descent, followed the duties of a fowler. But after knowing that he was son of a such and such king, he gave up his duties and followed the ways of his ancestors.[22] Another parable is explained to show the necessity of a teacher for enlightenment. Śaṅkarācārya writes that a teacher who is extremely sympathetic would free the individual who is carried away by the sensual pleasures of this world, just as a man who was brought up by robbers with eyes bounded from Gāndhāra region can go back home only if freed by a sympathetic person who directs him after removing his bandage.[23] In the same way, Śaṅkarācārya has given a number of analogies and parables relating to cities, rivers and persons to explain the nature of the knowledge of *Brahman* and the way to attain it.

22. *Bṛhadāraṇyaka Upaniṣad Bhāṣya*, 2.1.20.
23. *Chāndogya Upaniṣad Bhāṣya*, 6.14.2. All the references relating to this commentary are from Ganganatha Jha, tr. *The Chāndogya Upaniṣad with the Commentary of Śaṅkara*, 1942.

13

Social Philosophy of Śaṅkarācārya

Doctrine of illusion (māyā-vāda) — refuted

Śaṅkarācārya is 'one of the greatest religious leaders' that India has ever produced.[1] Some scholars have considered his monistic interpretation of Vedānta as the 'illusionist monism'.[2] This consideration is due to Śaṅkara's way of life, his criticism of *karma-kāṇḍa* (the path of actions), his analysis of *avidyā* (ignorance), *adhyāsa* (superimposition) of the individual and the doctrine of *māyā* as discussed by the writers of the Vedāntic tradition. But the commentaries of Śaṅkarācārya on the *prasthānatrayī* did not accord to the Illusionism. This wrong notion might be the result of the importance given to the said concepts by the historians of Indian philosophy neglecting the other side of the works of Śaṅkara.

The famous historian of Indian philosophy, S.N. Dasgupta while discussing the idea of superimposition (*adhyāsa*) and the influence of Gauḍapāda on Śaṅkarācārya, maintains that the belief in pure self as *sat-cit-ānanda* leads to accept that 'the world as it appears could not be real'. Hence, he says: 'For, if the self is what is ultimately real, the necessary conclusion is that all else is mere illusion or *māyā*'.[3] But, in-between these two statements, Dasgupta has not forgotten to state Śaṅkara's position, he writes:

---

1. Monier-Williams, *Religious Thought and Life in India*, 1978, p. 55.
2. For example, see Charles, A. Moore, ed., *The Indian Mind*, 1967, p. 8.
3. S.N. Dasgupta, *A History of Indian Philosophy*, vol. I, 1975, p. 435.

> Śaṅkara never tries to prove that the world is *māyā*, but accepts it as an indisputable.[4]

If the world and everything in it are unreal, there is no need for Śaṅkara to write commentaries, to travel the whole India and to establish monasteries. A great intellectual like Śaṅkara does not say that the world is unreal, but on the other hand, experience in the world and what we perceive around us cease to exist after some time. (In our existential condition everything around us is real; but at the same time the external world around us changes from age to age, and ultimately or historically at one time it ceases. It does not mean that the world is unreal, but the world of multiplicity changes and vanishes from era to era.) Therefore, the conclusion should be the world appearance is false, illusion and momentary, but not the actual world which is the effect of *Brahman*. The aim and goal of the teachings and writings of Śaṅkara is not to prove the unreality of the world or to exhibit the illusory-world, but to ascertain the meaning of the passages of the Upaniṣads in order to help people for attainment of liberation (*mokṣa*). There is much debate on superimposition (*adhyāsa*) and ignorance (*avidyā*) by Śaṅkara but not on illusion or *māyā*.[5]

However, the historians of Indian philosophy have allotted more pages to discuss the concept and nature of *māyā* in their books. It is also a fact that many Indian writers, either to their adherence to the Vedānta of Śaṅkara or over enthusiasm of completing their books have not made critical attempt to carry out the difference among the words: *adhyāsa*, *avidyā* and *māyā*. Of course, the recent writer of Indian philosophy, R. Puligandla has made a considerable effort in this direction.[6] With reference to the doctrine of *māyā*, the great authority on Vedānta, Paul Deussen has neither allotted a section nor discussed *māyā* as a

---

4. *A History of Indian Philosophy*, p. 435.
5. For further understanding see Karl. H. Potter, ed., *The Encyclopaedia of Indian Philosophies*, vol. III, 1981, pp. 32-4, 68-70, 78-80.
6. *Vide* his, *Fundamentals of Indian Philosophy*, 1985, pp. 216-20.

doctrine.[7] Significantly, Gaṅgānātha Jhā's English translation, the *Chāndogya Upaniṣad Bhāṣya* with the commentary of Śaṅkara, does neither contain any specific section entitled *māyā* in the introduction nor the word do found place in the index.[8] Similarly, Swāmī Mādhavānanda's translation of *The Bṛhadāraṇyaka Upaniṣad with the Commentary of Śaṅkarācārya* does not possess a vivid description of *māyā* doctrine.[9] T.M.P. Mahadevan, who has done extensive research in Advaita classics, has quoted a number of passages from the *Māṇḍūkya Kārikā Bhāṣya* to explain the concept of *māyā* and the status of the world, with an exception of a few from the *Brahma Sūtra Bhāṣya*.[10] This shows that the original commentaries on the *prasthānatrayī* did not have much information and discussion on *māyā* and world-illusion. But those who call Śaṅkara's non-dualism as illusionism are mostly writers who studied the histories of Indian Philosophy rather than the commentaries or the original works of Śaṅkara. Thus books written by authentic researchers and experts do not agree with the treatment given by the historians and writers of Indian philosophy on *māyā*.

Picking up the doctrine of illusion (*māyā*) of the world, some thinkers and writers have denied the relevance of any discussion on the ethics of Vedānta. A materialistic interpreter of Indian philosophy compared Advaita Vedānta with *śūnya-vādin*'s view of the world; and he concludes that 'the material world is just void or nothingness (*śūnya*)' or according to them 'the material world does not exist'.[11] Therefore the followers of Vedānta have tried to rectify this belief. For example, while discussing the ethical practices and ordinary values of life as asserted in Indian

---

7. Paul Deussen, *The System of Vedānta*, 1972, pp. vii-xiii.
8. Gaṅgānātha Jhā, *The Chāndogya Upaniṣad, with the Commentary of Śaṅkara*; 1942.
9. Swāmī Mādhavānanda, tr., *The Bṛhadāraṇyaka Upaniṣad, with the Commentary of Śaṅkarācārya*, 1965.
10. T.M.P. Mahadevan, *Śaṅkarācārya*, 1968, pp. 88-9.
11. Debi Prasad Chattopadhyaya, *What is Living and What is Dead in Indian Philosophy*, 1976, p. 47.

spirituality, Swāmī Nikhilānanda justifies the relevance of social values in Śaṅkara's Vedānta. Even by accepting the doctrine of *māyā* and the two levels of reality — *vyāvahārika* and *pāramārthika*, he concludes that 'social values cannot be denied by those who regard themselves as part of the relative world'.[12]

The whole system of Śaṅkarācārya has been discussed keeping in view the doctrine of *māyā* and the status of the empirical world. On the basis of these assumptions scholars derived their explanations and conclusions of pessimistic nature. Strictly speaking, it is the one-sided explanation of Advaita Vedānta; and does not contain the foundations of Vedānta. To repeat, it is a view that developed on the basis of taking some words and examples avoiding and forgetting the many sentences those advocated an optimistic view of life, an ethical code of conduct and a full realisation of human personality, the state of *jīvanmukta*. Apart from his metaphysical view of life, Śaṅkara has also subscribed to sociological outlook with reference to social order and moral behaviour. Therefore the point to remember is that *māyā* should neither be understood as illusion nor unreal, but unknowableness.

Social order

In the *Bṛhadāraṇyaka Upaniṣad Bhāṣya*, while commenting upon the evolution of the Universe from *virāj*, Śaṅkarācārya explains that the four castes originated — from the mouth of the cosmic vital force the brāhmaṇa caste, from arms the kṣatriyas, from thighs the vaiśyas, and from the feet the śūdras. So, Śaṅkara points out that the brāhmaṇas have strength in their mouth, kṣatriyas in physical body, while the strength of the vaiśyas and śūdras lies in agriculture and serving others respectively.[13] Śaṅkara mentions the Niṣādas as the fifth caste, which also constitutes a part of *Brahman*.[14]

---

12. Swāmī Nikhilānanda, 'The Realistic Aspect of Indian Spirituality' in C.A. Moore, *op. cit.*, p. 232.
13. *Bṛhadāraṇyaka Upaniṣad Bhāṣya*, 1.4.6.
14. *Ibid.*, 4.4.17.

Discussing the necessity of caste, life stage and actions, Śaṅkara asserts that 'the division of castes has been introduced in order to defend the undertaking of rites by people who are under ignorance. . . .'[15] The division of castes is a prerequisite for one to be righteous, if not one cannot perform appropriate rites.[16] In the introduction to the *Brahma-Sūtra-Bhāṣya*, Śaṅkarācārya says:

> Still (a knowledge of) the absolute Reality, that is the Self . . . is beyond hunger and thirst, free from such differentiation as brāhmaṇa, kṣatriya, etc., and is not subject to birth and death. And scriptures, which are operative before the dawn of the real knowledge of the dependence on, people grouping in ignorance. To illustrate the point: Such scriptural injunction as 'A brāhmaṇa shall perform a sacrifice' can become effective only by taking for granted various kinds of superimposition of caste, stage of life, age, condition, etc., And we said that superimposition means the cognition of something as some other thing.[17]

From this, it follows that the castes and stages of life and rites are relevant to ignorant people only. After the rise of self-knowledge, their utility ceases. Yet, one superimposes the characteristics of the body and senses on the self; and in the same way connects family and everything else to it. To this extent Śaṅkarācārya says in the *Bṛhadāraṇyaka Upaniṣad Bhāṣya:*

> The different castes such as the brāhmaṇa or the kṣatriya, the various orders of life and so on — upon which rites depend and which consist of actions and their factors and results, are objects of notions superimposed on the Self by ignorance, i.e., based on false notions like that of a snake in a rope.[18]

---

15. *Bṛhadāraṇyaka Upaniṣad Bhāṣya*, 1.4.15.
16. *Ibid.*, 1.4.14.
17. *Brahma-Sūtra-Bhāṣya*, Preamble or Harmony (*samanvaya*).
18. *Bṛhadāraṇyaka Upaniṣad Bhāṣya*, 2.4.5.

Thus as long as ignorance prevails, caste and life stage with their duties will continue. At another place Śaṅkarācārya points out that the Self acts like a dam to 'prevent the castes, colour, etc., from getting intermixed'.[19]

Śaṅkarācārya says that the scheme of castes and stages of life and everything that is connected with it, originates in the same way in every creation.[20] The *Taittirīya Upaniṣad Bhāṣya* accepts the validity of the caste system:

> If a man thinks, '*Brahman* is non-existence', then that man, by his want of faith, apprehends the entire righteous path, consisting of the scheme of castes, stages of life, etc., as false (non-existing), inasmuch as that path is not calculated to lead him to *Brahman*. Hence, this atheist is called as at, unrighteous in this world. As opposed to such a man, if any one who knows that '*Brahman* does exist', then, he, because of his faith, accepts truly the righteous path, comprising the scheme of castes, stages of life, etc., and leading to the realisation of *Brahman*.[21]

Śaṅkarācārya accepts the scriptural position regarding the various duties of different castes. For example, śūdras are debarred from *Brahman*-knowledge. While the three upper castes have the right of making a newborn baby licking the clarified butter with the means of a gold ring in the post-natal ceremony, the śūdras have no such right.[22] The brāhmaṇas are mentioned as 'the best among the twice born' and a brāhmaṇa is an 'earthly-god'.[23] Monastic life is open to them only and forbidden to other castes:

> the injunctions of the Śruti about the life long performance of rites concerned the other two castes except the

19. *Brahma-Sūtra-Bhāṣya,* 1.3.16.
20. *Ibid.*, 1.3.30.
21. *Taittirīya Upaniṣad Bhāṣya,* 2.6.1.
22. *Bṛhadāraṇyaka Upaniṣad Bhāṣya*, 1.5.2.
23. *Ibid.*, 5.14.1; *Brahma-Sūtra-Bhāṣya*, 3.3.8.

brāhmaṇa, for the kṣatriya and the vaiśyas are not entitled to the monastic life.[24]

However the three upper castes are equally qualified for the study of Vedas.[25] While commenting upon Gautama's learning from king Pravahana Jaivāli, Śaṅkarācārya states that in the ancient times brāhmaṇas used to learn knowledge from kṣatriyas or vaiśyas, and kṣatriyas from vaiśyas.[26]

Refuting the view that the life-stages are only three, Śaṅkarācārya says that they are four, i.e., the student, house holder, forest-dweller and monk, after considering a quotation from the *Jābāla Upaniṣad.*[27] In the *Chāndogya Upaniṣad Bhāṣya* an account of life-stages have been found. It states that the duties of sacrifice, study and charity are meant for the householder. The second kind of duties, austerity, etc., is meant for the ascetic, a wandering mendicant, who has not yet realised *Brahman.* The third kind of duties is prescribed for the life long religious student. They consist in service of the teacher throughout life, by residing with him and mortifying one's body through fasts and penances.[28]

Śaṅkarācārya asserts that any person in any life-stage can attain immortality if he rests firmly in *Brahman* by meditating upon *oṁ*. He says that the true knowledge of *Brahman* is impossible to get for those who possess the notion of duality. Men of dualism (*dvaitavādin*s) see things differently and their ideas are false and wrong. Therefore, a man who has not disassociates himself from the notion of duality (*dvaita-bhāva*) and actions (*karma*s), could not be grounded firmly in *Brahman.* He also says that there is no possibility of disassociation from actions (*karma*s) in other life-stages, except in the state of *saṁnyāsa*, the renunciation. Neither the householder nor the wandering mendicant, who merely wanders in search of alms,

---

24. *Bṛhadāraṇyaka Upaniṣad Bhāṣya*, 4.5.15.
25. *Ibid.*, 4.4.22.
26. *Ibid.*, 6.2.7.
27. *Brahma-Sūtra-Bhāṣya*, 3.4.20.
28. *Chāndogya Upaniṣad Bhāṣya*, 2.23.1.

can not be regarded as one who 'rests firmly in *Brahman*'. But a wandering mendicant, who enters upon the final life-stage and who disassociates himself from all actions and their result will be he who 'rests firmly in *Brahman*'; and he alone attains immortality. He is called *paramahaṁsa*.

Śaṅkarācārya says that those persons who fail to follow the duties of their life-stage are to be expelled from society; and others should not have relations with them in connection with sacrifices, study and marriage alliances.[29] Thus, people are expected to follow their duties as per the life-stage and caste as stated by the scriptures. Śaṅkara also affirms the prohibition of the performance of another's duty:

> Logic also supports this: for one's own duty is that which has been prescribed (by the scriptures) for one, and not what one can perform well, since duty is determined by scriptural injunction.[30]

It is also said that if a person strictly follows his own duty, he gets high reward. Śaṅkara says that the Smr̥ti literature asserts this:

> People belonging to the different castes and stages of life, who sincerely perform their duties, experience the fruits of their works after death, and then through the residual *karma* get births amidst special environment and have special caste, family, outstanding beauty, long life, knowledge, good conduct, wealth, happiness and intelligence.[31]

Ethics

According to Śaṅkarācārya man becomes responsible and desires to direct his conduct when there is a possibility of reaping the consequences of his actions. He says:

---

29. *Brahma-Sūtra-Bhāṣya*, 3.4.43.
30. *Br̥hadāraṇyaka Upaniṣad Bhāṣya*, 3.4.40.
31. *Ibid.*, 3.1.

> In any case, a man who believes that there is a self which gets into relations with a future body, seeks to know the particular means of attaining the good and avoiding the evil in connection with that body.[32]

The conviction of transmigration and eternity of the self results in the search for the good. Only correct understanding helps one to know what is good and what is bad. This can be attained through understanding of scriptural passages only.[33] Commenting on the story of the sons of Prajāpati, gods and devils those struggled with each other for this world, Śaṅkara comments that Prajāpati is nothing but one's own personality in which the struggle takes place. If the scriptures influence one's thought, speech and action, one becomes a god. But if ignorance or natural tendencies influence one, one becomes a devil. Thus in all human beings there is a struggle between natural tendencies and the scriptural path; each of them struggles to suppress the other. Therefore, Śaṅkara points out, gods are few since cultivation of one's personality by the scriptures is rare, and is to be attained with a great effort.[34]

Similarly a passage of the *Bṛhadāraṇyaka Upaniṣad* states that Prajāpati had three kinds of offspring — gods, men and devils. He instructed them to practice self-control, charity and compassion respectively. On this Śaṅkarācārya observes that, there are no gods or devils other than men. Among men, those who have self-control are gods, and those who are greedy are men while those who injure others are devils. Therefore, the import of this Upaniṣadic passage is as follows:

> Hence it is men who should learn all the three instructions, for Prajāpati meant his advice for them alone; because men are observed to be wild, greedy and cruel.[35]

---

32. *Bṛhadāraṇyaka Upaniṣad Bhāṣya*, Introduction 1.1.1.
33. *Ibid.*, 1.3.1.
34. *Ibid.*; *Chāndogya Upaniṣad Bhāṣya,* 1.2.1.
35. *Bṛhadāraṇyaka Upaniṣad Bhāṣya*, 5.2.3.

According to Śaṅkarācārya, the aim of Vedānta is to bring the identity of individual self with the Supreme Self, *Brahman*. It is an ideal for man. Śaṅkara says that it is liberation or immortality. It is not something to be achieved since immortality is the very nature of the self. It is realisation (*aṇu vedanā*) which is possible in this very life.[36] Śaṅkara says that the liberated man, who identifies himself with all and considering all as *Brahman*, is *jīvanmukta*.[37]

Śaṅkarācārya points out that ignorance is the opposite of that leads to liberation. Ignorance has roots in desire, due to it men are attached to family, property, etc. Sorrow comes to men when the individual self is identified with the body.[38] As long as a person is associated with limiting adjuncts like the body, etc., he needs prohibition and injunction. At that level Śaṅkara accepts the usual sort of ethics found in the Śruti and Dharmaśāstras:

> One shall approach one's wife at the proper time . . .
> One shall not approach one's teacher's wife . . .
> One shall sacrifice an animal to Agni and Soma . . .
> One shall not injure any being . . .
> One shall entertain one's friend . . .
> One shall avoid one's enemy.[39]

Śaṅkarācārya says that the scheme of castes, life stages, etc., tending to *Brahman* realisation constitutes the righteous path; those who follow it are good people.[40] Everyone ought to perform the duties pertaining to his caste and stage in life; the *saṁnyāsin*s (renunciates) have, of course, no duties. For śūdras there are no *āśrama*s or life stages; and *saṁnyāsa* is only for brāhmaṇas. Apart from caste duties, the practice of celibacy, austerity, truthfulness, control of senses and non-injury are auxiliaries in

36. *Taittirīya Upaniṣad Bhāṣya*, 1.11.4; *Kena Upaniṣad Bhāṣya*, 2.4; *Bṛhadāraṇyaka Upaniṣad Bhāṣya*, 4.4.8
37. *Bṛhadāraṇyaka Upaniṣad Bhāṣya,* 4.4.6-7; *Bhagavad Gītā Bhāṣya*, 6.27.
38. *Brahma-Sūtra-Bhāṣya*, 2.3.46.
39. *Ibid.*, 2.3.48.
40. *Taittirīya Upaniṣad Bhāṣya*, 2.6.1.

all the life stages.[41] While commenting upon the discussion of Yājñavalkya with some brāhmaṇas in the court of king Janaka, Śaṅkara observes that one should not be disrespectful to the knower of *Brahman* but be submissive to him.[42]

In connection with the killing of animals in sacrifices, Śaṅkara explains that the scripture is the only source of knowledge to decide what is good and what is bad. Without scriptural guidance, people are incapable of deciding the morality of any action or deed, since it depends upon space, time and environment, for a virtuous action performed in a particular situation, time and place may not be so in another context, time and place. Conse quently, Śaṅkara is of the opinion that an individual cannot rely on himself for the knowledge of good and bad.[43]

The Vedānta metaphysics, though related to the trans cendental world, had bearing on the phenomenal world and social life with its empirical remarks and references. Śaṅkarācārya says that great people who were endowed with peace shall work for the world's welfare, and remarks that humility and non-hatredness constitutes the nature of *Brahman*-knower, which implies an ethical life of high order in the society. Professor K. Satchidananda Murty says that the doctrine of *Brahman* and *ātman* and the assertion of *Brahman* as the inner-self of all beings imply equality and equanimity in practical world.[44] In tune with this social philosophy of Śaṅkara, a remark in a latest research work on Vedānta is worth noticing:

> The metaphysics of Vedanta cannot cohere with any kind of thinking which admits that some races, classes or individuals are superior to others, or that any groups or individuals have inherent privileges not open to all others.[45]

---

41. *Taittirīya Upaniṣad Bhāṣya*, 1.11.4.
42. *Bṛhadāraṇyaka Upaniṣad Bhāṣya*, 3.9.26.
43. *Brahma-Sūtra-Bhāṣya*, 3.1.25.
44. K. Satchidananda Murty, 'What we owe to Śaṅkara' in R. Balasubramanian and Sibajian Bhattacharya, ed., *Perspectives of Śaṅkara*, 1989, p. 444.
45. P. George Victor, *op cit.*, p. 207.

14

Interpretations on Śaṅkarācārya

In recent times academicians with an extensive research work and many debates have interpreted the philosophy of Śaṅkarācārya. So far, the identity of *ātman* and *Brahman*, the concept of *jīvanmukta* and the illusory status of the world and falsity in human cognition have been thought of as the fundamental doctrines of Advaita Vedānta. This kind of subjective aspect has been expounded as the philosophy of Śaṅkara limiting to some metaphysical and epistemological doctrines. But on the contrary various scholars have interpreted Vedānta of Śaṅkara in different ways in contemporary times from the objective spirit. Subscribing to this spirit Duncan Greenless wrote the life of Śaṅkara in 1953 for the first time in the introduction to his *The Gospel of Advaita*.[1] Duncan Greenless in this pioneering work brought out how Śaṅkara's own ideals have been practised in his personal life. He has mentioned a number of minor works such as *Vivekacūḍāmaṇi*, *Tattvopadeśa*, *Harigotra*, *Ātma-bodha* and *Aparokṣānubhūti* ascribed to Śaṅkara. He also maintains that the great books, *The Yoga-vāśiṣṭha* and *Patañjala Yoga-sūtras* are also the sources for the gospel of Advaita.[2]

T.M.P. Mahadevan, an *advaitin* by temperament and training who has done intensive research on Advaita classics has authored a book called *Śaṅkarācārya* published in 1968[3] by projecting the philosophy and life of Śaṅkara. This book analysed the philosophy

---

1. Duncan Greenless, *The Gospel of Advaita*, 1953, pp. xxi-i.
2. *Ibid.*, p. cii.
3. *Vide* his book, *Śaṅkarācārya*, 1968, pp. 1-43.

of Śaṅkara by co-ordinating the religious activity with the spiritual life. T.M.P. Mahadevan has projected Śaṅkara as a *prasanna-gambhīra*, lucid and deep in metaphysical writings and showing the way to spiritual sanity in practical life.[4]

The subsequent writings and research articles have projected and analysed the various perspectives of Śaṅkarācārya and are published as articles in books. This activity has gone beyond the metaphysical teachings of Śaṅkara to the other aspects of his life. A study of these perspectives gives the total picture of Śaṅkara as a devotee, *yogī* and pragmatic thinker with reference to Vedic way of life.

Devotional aspects

T.M.P. Mahadevan has interpreted Śaṅkarācārya as a devotee and he has translated a number of hymns attributed to Śaṅkara. In general it may be argued that when the individual self is one with the Supreme Self by realising non-duality, there shall not be any place for worship and devotion. If there is a difference, there would be a devotee and deity for the non-dualist there shall not be any religious and devotional practices. Keeping this view in mind, T.M.P. Mahadevan says that in the phenomenal existence the individual self certainly believes that there is god (*Īśvara*) who is creator of the universe and tries to take up whatever the necessary means to realise and reach god. Though Advaita Vedānta admits oneness of individual self and Supreme Self, there is also a distinction that cannot be forgotten. T.M.P. Mahadevan says that the Supreme Self is like a sea and the individual self is the wave of the sea. It means the wave belongs to the sea, but not the sea to the wave. Similarly, the individual self belongs to the Supreme Self but not the Supreme Self to individual self. Thus, in the phenomenal existence, devotion is accepted to reach the state of non-duality. The exclusive importance given to the path of knowledge (*jñāna-mārga*) by Śaṅkara does not mean that Śaṅkara has denied the role of devotion in the empirical standpoint and gave permission to the

4. *Śaṅkarācārya*, p. 58.

masses by forgetting their duties and responsibilities. Therefore, though belief in the personal god is not related to the highest state but it is relevant to the masses those who cannot reach the highest state. T.M.P. Mahadevan writes: 'Devotion to *Īśvara* is a necessary step to Advaita-realisation'.[5] He remarks that the life-mission of Śaṅkara is to remove the differences among faiths by purifying their modes of worship and approaches to God, similar to his Advaita which aims to remove the difference between the individual self and Supreme Self.

P. Nagaraja Rao is also of the opinion that devotion as a popular mode of worship has been accepted by Śaṅkarācārya. A critical study of the commentaries of Śaṅkara reveals, he says, that one cannot realise or reach the *pāramārthika-satya* (the highest level) suddenly transcending the *vyāvahārika-satya* (the empirical level). Man has to necessarily experience the differences at the empirical level. Naga-raja Rao says that for ordinary man Śaṅkara has advocated 'a graded path' which helps the seeker to rise step by step in which devotion has its place. He remarks:

> Advaita religion has a definite place of *bhakti*, Śaṅkarācārya does not downgrade *bhakti*. ... Śaṅkara has huge volume of great devotional poetry to his credit.[6]

By writing a number of hymns to various gods, Nagaraja Rao says, and by starting the *pañcāyatana-pūjā*, Śaṅkarācārya enunciated the role of *bhakti* in realising the Absolute. The different names given to Śaṅkara such as *jagad-guru*, *ṣaṇmata-sthāpanācārya* proves that Śaṅkara has admitted worship and devotion by denying the differences among the cults and difference in-between man and God.

Nagaraja Rao says that devotion in Śaṅkara is a method that directs the mode of mind towards God constantly and leads man's mind to get absorbed itself in God. According to Śaṅkara, he says, devotion is like the love of a woman to her husband and

---

5. T.M.P. Mahadevan, *The Hymns of Śaṅkara*, 1980, p. 31.
6. P. Nagaraja Rao, *Fundamentals of Indian Philosophy*, p. 121.

the flow of a river to the ocean. *Bhakti* in Śaṅkara is associated with true spirituality and sincerity with ethical excellence. Thus, *bhakti* is not explicit but implicit in the nature of man; it is not worship in temples but an inward prayer, and deep devotion to God. P. Nagaraja Rao has quoted a number of verses from the hymns of Śaṅkara especially from *Bhaja-Govindam* and *Viṣṇu-sahasra-nāma*, those contains aspects of *bhakti*. A devotee should be a man of modest nature who subdues his mind and sympathetic for the living beings. Śaṅkara denies the ritual and religious acts such as offering flowers and fruits associated with devotion. The devotee should concentrate on the Lord with spiritual commitment and self-control.

Devotion is not an outward activity but an inner attitude of the mind and a complete surrender to God. Śaṅkarācārya says that by worshipping God and by praying to God one transcends the phenomenal state and reaches perfection, which is spiritual. A number of hymns addressed to Lord Śiva, Lord Viṣṇu, Lord Kṛṣṇa and Lord Kāśī Viśvanātha gave ample evidence that Śaṅkara holds devotion (*bhakti*) as a necessary step to reach perfection, *pāramārthika-satya* (the highest level).[7]

D.N. Shanbag in his article 'Śaṅkarācārya — The Great Devotee of Lord Viṣṇu'[8] argues that Śaṅkara is a devotee, and equated Lord Viṣṇu with *Brahman* of Śaṅkara. Śaṅkara in his commentaries mentioned 'Nārāyaṇa' as the controller of the Universe being *Antaryāmin* (inner being) and therefore Shanbag says that in the *Viṣṇu Purāṇa*, Nārāyaṇa has been interpreted as Supreme Lord; and all the scriptural teachings asserted the same.[9] Further, the study of the *Bhagavad Gītā Bhāṣya*, Shanbag says, reveals the fact that the Supreme Being is Viṣṇu or Nārāyaṇa, according to Śaṅkara. He interprets that Śaṅkara calls the 'illusion of the Supreme Being' as Vaiṣṇava *māyā* and

---

7. P. Nagaraja Rao, *op. cit.*, pp. 122-3.
8. R. Balasubramanian and Sibajiban Bhattacharya, ed., *Perspectives of Śaṅkara*, 1989, pp. 317-29.
9. *Ibid.*, p. 323.

critique of those who considered Viṣṇu to be the inferior God. Following are some references quoted by Shanbhag from the *Bhagavad Gītā Bhāṣya* of Śaṅkara:[10]

(i) *prakṛtim svam mama vaiṣṇavim māyām* — iv.6

(ii) *kaṭham-punardaivim-etam triguṇātmikam vaisṇavim māyāmatikrānti* — vii.14

(iii) *yanti modyajino madyajanasila vaiṣṇava mameva yanti* — ix.25

In addition to these verses, several names of Viṣṇu given by Śaṅkara in the commentaries on Upaniṣads and Gauḍapāda *Kārikā* prove the fact that Śaṅkara was a devotee to Lord Viṣṇu. Shanbag says that the author of *Nārāyaṇīyam*, Meppattur Nārāyaṇa Bhaṭṭattiri who lived in the beginning of the seventeenth century AD has mentioned that Śaṅkara was a devotee to Viṣṇu apart from his devotion to other gods. The biographer of Śaṅkara, Mādhava who wrote the *Śaṅkara-dig-vijaya* has mentioned that at the time of death of his mother, Śaṅkara has recited one hymn in praise of Lord Śiva and another in praise of Mahā Viṣṇu.[11]

Prabhakar Apte of Deccan College, Pune in his article, remarked that Śaṅkara's practical religious activity has richly contributed for the growth of socio-religious life of India.[12] It is a fact that the Temple building activity was advanced by the followers of Rāmānuja; but the *pañcāyatana-pūjā* advocated by Śaṅkara and his followers has become a boon in disguise for the flourishing development of temple building activity in India,[13] as the *pañcāyatana-pūjā* involves accommodation of five deities, Śiva, Viṣṇu, Gaṇapati, Sūrya and Śakti in one temple complex that gave rise to a practical basis for meditation and worship. Thus by providing a theoretical basis for the worship in tune with the oneness of all gods under the state of *saguṇa* Brahma

10. *Perspectives of Śaṅkara*, p. 328.
11. *Ibid.*, p. 324.
12. *Ibid.*, pp. 340-5.
13. *Ibid.*, p. 343.

and also the supremacy of *Brahman* in all of them, Śaṅkara's Advaita Vedānta has promoted to a great extent the cultural life of India.

Active social work

Researches on the role and place of Śaṅkarācārya have been enunciated in contemporary times. Not only Śaṅkara's metaphysical ideas but also practical norms are being examined critically because he has raised the status of man by interpreting the divine nature in him (*tat tvam asi*). By advocating the path of knowledge (*jñāna-mārga*) Śaṅkara has liberated man from rituals and sacrifices. This is something that effected the social life of the individual and society. It is said that by establishing the four religious monasteries in the four corners of India, Śaṅkara has visualised the national integration and solidarity of the country. Through his aim and religious perspective, the four monasteries gave rise a conception of unity in practical life.

Swāmī Vivekānanda for the first time in the history of India has reinterpreted the Vedānta of Śaṅkarācārya as 'Practical Vedānta'. With an intimate knowledge of various movements such as socialism and communism, Swāmī Vivekānanda has advanced the practical effects of the theoretical metaphysics of Vedānta. His views are published in the form of a book called *Caste, Culture and Socialism*, by the Advaita Ashram, Calcutta in 1978.

Swāmī Vivekānanda says that there should not be any privileges for one caste; and he felt that the duty of the brāhmaṇa is 'to work for the salvation of the rest of mankind in India'.[14] He says that modern caste distinction is a barrier to India's progress as it separates people. The oneness of Supreme *Brahman* and the individual *ātma* and the appearance of *Brahman* in all beings equally imply that all men are one in God. He says that human equality and universal brotherhood are the true spirit of Advaita Vedānta. Therefore Vivekānanda says:

---

14. Swāmī Vivekānanda, *Caste, Culture and Socialism*,1989, p. 47.

> The caste system is opposed to the religion of Vedānta.
> We must give up the idea of privilege . . . .
> the idea that one man is superior to
> another has no meaning in the Vedanta.[15]

The positive place of Śaṅkarācārya in Indian history has been assessed by Professor Hiltrud Rustau[16] of Humboldt University, Berlin. She says that Śaṅkara's philosophy includes many implications, fundamentally while the twice-born enjoyed the privileges, Śaṅkara enunciated the impermanence of world's reality[17]. Śaṅkara's philosophy, according to Hiltrud Rustau, provides 'the humanistic implications of the Vedanta philosophy by developing out of its structure, the philosophical explanation of the equality of man and the demand for charity as well as for active social work, in the hands of Raja Rammohun Roy, who 'stressed the equality of the Indians and their religions, thus rejecting the activities of the Christian missionaries'.[18] Professor Hiltrud Rustau says that Vivekānanda developed a comprehensive social concept based on Advaita Vedānta. She writes:

> If Ramakrishna had mainly stressed the equality of religions, Vivekananda, continuing this line of thinking, developed out of the main positions of Śaṅkara's philosophy the demand for equality of human beings. Especially he used the idea of each man's individuality and of the unity of the universe contained in Śaṅkara's philosophy.[19]

Starting from the *tat tvam asi* (that thou art) and, *aham brahmāsmi* (I am *Brahman*) sentences of the Upaniṣads,

---

15. *Caste, Culture and Socialism*, pp. 31, 43.
16. Hiltrud Rustau 'The Place of Sankaracharya in Indian Philosophy', in R. Balasubramanian and Sibajian Bhattacharya, ed., *Perspectives of Śaṅkara*, 1989, pp. 382-92.
17. *Ibid.*, p. 384.
18. *Ibid.*, p. 385.
19. *Ibid.*, p. 386.

continued in the Advaita interpretation of Śaṅkarācārya, the metaphysics of Vedānta was turned by Swāmī Vivekānanda towards the social aspects of society. Thus the 'Practical Vedānta' has emerged by resolving the contradiction between Śaṅkara's metaphysics and his ethics in accordance with non-dualism (Advaita). Professor Hiltrud Rustau has quoted a number of sentences and sayings regarding Vivekānanda's concern for equality of human beings, suppressed masses, and universal-brotherhood. She remarks that Advaita (non-duality) has been the underlying principle of Vivekānanda's interpretation of Vedānta. She concludes:

> Thus Vivekananda on the basis of Sankara's philosophical concept developed a thorough humanist social philosophy responding to the demands of his time.[20]

Professor K. Satchidananda Murty has pioneered the type of research that estimates the place of Śaṅkarācārya 'in cultural history of the country and spiritual life of our nation'. In his article, 'What We Owe to Śaṅkara', Satchidananda Murty remarks that Śaṅkara's missionary zeal and his establishment of monasteries influenced the national leaders and political thinkers to conceive national integration and oneness of the people. He says that when Vedic knowledge, and its study is limited to upper castes or when the knowledge of the transcendental truth is limited to the higher castes, Śaṅkara has brought out a revolution by introducing the *sādhana-catuṣṭaya* as the only four prerequisites to learn *Brahman*-knowledge (*brahma-vidyā*). Śaṅkara made it possible that 'caste and occupation are not criterion for *brahma-vidyā*'.[21] Another revolutionary aspect that Śaṅkara brought in the traditional life of the religious people against the Dharmaśāstra view of life is that one need not go through all the life-stages in order to become a mendicant (*saṁnyāsin*). After leading the state of *brahmacarya*, Śaṅkara straight away became a *saṁnyāsin*; and subsequently

---

20. *Perspectives of Śaṅkara*, p. 388.
21. K. Satchidananda Murty's article in R. Balasubramanian and Sibajiban Bhattacharya, ed., *op. cit.*, p. 443.

being a *saṁnyāsin* he performed the funeral rite of his mother as per her wish. This is something according to Satchidananda Murty the triumph of wisdom and reason with reference to human values against taboos and conventions. Śaṅkara in his life was questioned by an outcast on the streets of Benāras. A story that connected with this incident tells when Śaṅkara shouted on the approach of an outcast to move away, the outcast asked Śaṅkara, whether he is saying to the self or body because the self in all is same according to Advaita. Śaṅkara being deeply shaken and surprised to the remark of the outcast realised and uttered five verses, each ends with the following last sentence:

cāṇḍālo'stu sa tu dvijo'stu
guru rityesa manisa mama.[22]

He who has such stead-fast-insight is my *guru*,
whether, he be an outcast or a Brāhmaṇa.
This is my firm understanding.

---

22. *Perspectives of Śaṅkara*, p. 444.

Glossary

ācārya : traditional teacher in theology, expert in crafts

adhyāsa : without cognition, superimposition

Advaita Vedānta : Non-dualism of Śaṅkarācārya

ahiṁsā : non-injury, non-violence

anirvacanīya : indefinable, indescribable

anumāna : inference

anupalabdhi : non-cognition

anurāga : compassion

anusandhāna : meditation, connecting two entities

apauruṣeya : not man-made

Āraṇyakas : forest-treatises of the Vedas

arthāpatti : postulation

Atharvaveda : the fourth Veda contains medical and magical formulas of practical life

ātma : individual/self

ātmā : soul

avatāra : incarnation

avidyā : ignorance

avirodha : non-conflict

bhakti : devotion

Brahma-loka : world of Brahman

Brahma-nirvāṇa : peaceful extinction in Brahman, God

Brahma-sākṣātkāra : vision of God, Brahman

Brahma-vādinī : discussant on Brahman

brahmacarya : traditionally the first-state of life acquiring Brahman-knowledge

Brahman : Absolute God, the omnipotent creator, the World-soul spoken in the Upaniṣads

brāhmaṇas : the first among the traditional four castes, ritual sections of the Vedas

Brahmānubhava : divine experience of Brahman

Devanāgarī : literally means 'related to the city of Gods', ancient Indian script, Hindi script

deva-yāna : way of the Gods

Dvaita Vedānta : Dualism of Madhvācārya

Gauḍapāda : author of the commentary on the *Māṇḍūkya Upaniṣad*, known as *Māṇḍūkya Kārikā*

gauṇa-pratyaya : figurative expression

gṛhasthāśrama : traditionally the second state of life, house-holder state

guṇa : trait, characteristic, quality

guru : teacher

guru-kulas : Vedic religious schools

Īśvara : personal God, Lower conception of Brahman

jagad-guru : world-teacher

jijñāsā : Inquiry into knowledge, desire to know truth

jīvan-mukta : liberated soul from bounds, while in living

jñāna-kāṇḍa : parts of the Vedas related to the path of knowledge

jñāna-mārga : the path of knowledge

jñāna-yoga : the discipline of devotion

jyotiṣam : astrology

kaivalya : liberation from worldly life

kalpa : ritual

kāmya-karmas : desired actions, rites intended for a purpose

karma-kāṇḍa : parts of the Vedas related to the path of rituals

karma-mārga : the path of actions, rituals

karma-yoga : the discipline of action.

kāvyas : Indian classics, epics

kṣatriyas : the second of the four traditional castes

loka-saṁgraha : welfare of the world

Lokāyatas : followers of materialistic life

mahā-vākya : great sentence

manana : Repetition, Remembering

Manu : the author of ancient Indian law code

māyā : illusion, non-cognition, unknowable

mithyā-pratyaya : illusory notion.

mokṣa : liberation from the world of suffering

naimittika-karmas : occasional rites

naiṣkarmya : renunciation of all actions

nidhidhyāsana : concentration, profound meditation

nimitta-mātra : mere instrument

nirguṇa : without traits, qualities

niruktam : etymology

nirvāṇa : enlightenment, peaceful extinction

nitya-karmas : regular actions, rites

nivṛtti : withdrawal, without motive to do

pañcāyatana-pūjā : worshiping a god out of five deities

paṇḍits : teachers in Indian scriptures and literature

paramahaṁsa-parivrājaka : prime position of the fourth-state of life

pāramārthika-satya : divine standpoint, highest state of truth

paramātman : Supreme soul, God

phala : fruit, result

pitṛ-yāna : way of the fathers

pradhāna : primordial, original substance

prakaraṇa-granthas : minor books of Śaṅkarācārya

prakaraṇam : chapter

pramāṇa : standard, criteria of knowledge

prasthāna-trayī : the three books — the Upaniṣads, *Bagavad Gītā* and *Brahma Sutra*

pratyakṣa : direct perception

pravṛtti : action, positive nature towards duties

prāyaścitta karmas : expiatory actions, rites

puruṣa : man, self, all-pervasive entity

Pūrva Mīmāṁsā : Vedic school of rituals

pūrva-pakṣa : earlier view, opponent's view

rajas : passion, desire, restless attitude

Ṛgveda : the first Veda, contains hymns in praise of deities

sādhana-catuṣṭaya : four-fold means, pre-requisites for Brahman-knowledge

saguṇa : positive trait, characteristic, quality

sākṣin : witness

samādhi : deep sleep state, end of consciousness

samanvaya : reconciliation

Sāmaveda : the third Veda, contains songs of responsive reading

saṁnyāsin : religious mendicant, traditionally related to the fourth state of life

saṁsāra : family life in the world

śāstras : scriptures

sattva : goodness, purity, being rational

Shah Jehan : the Mughal Emperor of Delhi

śikṣā : phonetics

śiṣya : disciple, student

ślokas : stanzas, verses

smṛti : that remembered, e.g., Manu law code

śravaṇa : listening

śruti : that heard, e.g., Vedas

stotras : hymns in praise of deities

śūdras : the fourth of the four traditional castes

svarga : heaven

tamas : ignorance, laziness

tattva-jñāna : real, absolute-knowledge

ṭīkā : glossary

timira : an eye disease like jaundice

upādhis : limiting adjuncts

upamāna : stories

upanayanam : traditional initiation ceremony of learning

upāsanā : wishful meditation

Uttara Mīmāṁsā : Vedic school of knowledge

vaidika : believer of Vedas, related to Vedic rituals

vairāgya : non-attachment

vaiśyas : the third of the four traditional castes

vānaprastha āśrama : traditionally the third state of life, forest dweller

Vedānta : related to the ending portions of the Vedas

vijaya : victory

vinaya : orderly, obedient

Viśiṣṭādvaita Vedānta: Qualified Non-dualism of Rāmānujācārya

vyākaraṇa : grammar

Vyāsa : the great ancient sage who wrote the Indian epics

vyāvahārika-satya : worldly stand point, empirical truth

Yajurveda : the second Veda, contains rules of rituals

yoga : meditation, discipline

Bibliography

Aurobindo, Sri, *Essays on the Gītā,* First Series, Calcutta: Arya Publishing House, 1944.

Bala Gangadhara Tilak, *Śrīmad Bhagavadgītā Rahasya*, Poona: Lokamanya Tilak Mandir, 1936.

Balasubramanian, R. and Sibajivan Bhattacharya, eds., *Perspectives of Śaṅkara*, New Delhi: Department of Culture, Govt. of India, 1989.

Belvalkar, S.K., *Vedānta Philosophy,* Part I, Poona: Bilva Kunja Publishing House, 1929.

Chandradhara Sharma, *A Critical Survey of Indian Philosophy*, Delhi: Motilal Banarsidass, 1976.

Chatterji, Mohini M., tr., *Viveka-cūḍāmaṇi*, Madras: Theosophical Publishing House, 1983.

Chattopadhyaya, D.P., *What is Living and What is Dead in Indian Philosophy*, New Delhi: Peoples Publishing House, 1976.

Colebrooke, H.T., *Essays on the Religion and Philosophy of the Hindus*, New Delhi: Ashok Publications, 1976.

Dasgupta, S.N., *A History of Indian Philosophy,* Delhi: Motilal Banarasidass, 1975.

Deussen, Paul, *The System of Vedānta*, Delhi: Motilal Banarasidass, 1972.

Devaraja, N.K, *An Introduction to Sankara's Theory of Knowledge*, Delhi: Motilal Banarsidass, 1972.

Desai, Mahadeva, *The Gītā According to Gandhi*, Ahmedabad: Navajivan Publishing House, 1951.

Edgerton, Franklin, tr., *The Bhagavad Gītā*, Part I, Cambridge, Mass: Harvard University Press, 1952.

Feinberg, Joel, *Social Philosophy*, Englewood Cliffs, New Jersey: Prentice Hall, Inc., 1973.

Gambhirananda, Swami, tr., *Eight Upaniṣads*, in Two Volumes, Calcutta: Advaita Ashram, 1978.

Gambhirananda, Swami, tr., *Brahma Sūtra Bhāṣya of Śrī Śaṅkarācārya*, Calcutta: Advaita Ashram, 1977.

Ganganatha Jha, tr., *The Chāndogya Upaniṣad with the Commentary of Śaṅkarācārya:* Poona: Oriental Book Agency, 1942.

George Victor, P., *Social Philosophy of Vedanta,* Calcutta: K.P. Bagchi and Company, 1991.

Greenless, Duncan, *The Gospel of Advaita*, Madras: The Theosophical Publishing House, 1953.

Hill, W. Douglas, P., tr., *The Bhagavad Gītā*, London: Oxford University Press, 1953.

Hume, R.E., *The Thirteen Principal Upanisads*, Madras: Oxford University Press, 1949.

Jagadananda, Swami, tr., *Upadeśa-sahasrī: A Thousand Teachings*, Madras: Sri Ramakrishna Math, 1979.

Keshava Menon, Y., *The Mind of Ādi Śaṅkara*, Bombay: Jaico Publishing House, 1976.

Madhavananda, Swami, tr., *The Bṛhadāraṇyaka Upaniṣad with the commentary of Śaṅkarācārya*, Calcutta: Advaita Ashrama, 1965.

Mahadevan, T.M.P., *Gauḍapāda: A Study in Early Advaita*, Madras: University of Madras Press, 1954.

Mahadevan, T.M.P., *The Philosophy of Advaita*, Madras: Ganesh & Co., Pvt. Ltd., 1957.

Mahadevan, T.M.P., *Śaṅkarācārya*, New Delhi: National Book Trust, India, 1968.

Mahadevan, T.M.P., ed., *The Preceptor's of Advaita*, Secunderabad: Sri Kanchi Kama Koti Sankaracarya Mandir, 1968.

Mahadevan, T.M.P., *The Hymns of Śaṅkara*, Delhi: Motilal Banarsidass, 1980.

Mahadeva Sastry, Alladi, tr., *The Bhagavad Gītā with the Commentary of Śrī Śaṅkarācārya*, Madras: Samata Books, 1977.

Mahadeva Sastry, Alladi, tr., *Dakṣiṇa-mūrti stotra*, Madras: Samata Books, 1978.

Moore, Charles A., ed., *The Indian Mind*, Honolulu: East-West Centre-Press, 1967.

Nagaraja Rao, P., *Fundamentals of Indian Philosophy*, New Delhi: Indian Book Company.

Nakamura, Hajime, *A History of Early Vedanta Philosophy,* Part I, Delhi: Motilal Banarsidass, 1983.

Nikhilananda, Swami, *Self-Knowledge*, Madras: Sri Ramakrishna Math, 1978.

Nilakanta Sastry, K.A., *A History of South India*, Madras: Oxford University Press, 1966.

Nilakanta Sastry, K.A. and G. Srinivasachari, *Life and Culture of the Indian People*, Bombay: Allied Publishers, 1974.

Panikkar, K.M., *A Survey of Indian History*, Bombay: Asia Publishing House, 1963.

Patrick, E.M. Kirk, ed., *Chambers 20th Century Dictionary*, Bombay: Allied Publishers, 1985.

Potter, Karl H., ed., *The Encyclopaedia of Indian Philosophies*, vol. III, Delhi: Motilal Banarsidass, 1981.

Prabhakara Machive, ed., *Bhāratīya Saṁskriti*, Calcutta: Bharatiya Samskrita Samsad, 1983.

Prabhavananda, Swami, *The Spiritual Heritage of India*, Madras: Sri Ramakrishna Math, 1977.

Puligandla, R., *Fundamentals of Indian Philosophy*, New Delhi: D.K. Printworld (P) Ltd., 1997.

Radhakrishnan, *Indian Philosophy,* vol.II, London: George Allen and Unwin Ltd., 1966.

Ranade, R.D., *A Constructive Survey of Upaniṣadic Philosophy*, Bombay: Bharatiya Vidya Bhavan, 1968.

Ranade, R.D., *Vedanta, The Culmination of Indian Thought*, Bombay: Bharatiya Vidya Bhavan, 1970.

Sankaranarayana, P., tr., *Viveka-cūḍāmaṇi*, Bombay: Bharatiya Vidya Bhavan, 1973.

Satchidananda Murty, K., *Revelation and Reason in Advaita Vedanta*, Delhi: Motilal Banarsidass, 1974.

Tapasyananda, Sri Swami, tr., *Śaṅkara-Dig-Vijaya: by Madhava-Vidyāraṇya,* Fifth Impression, Madras: Sri Ramakrishna Math.

Thapar, Romila, *A History of India,* Volume One, Middlesex, England: Penguin Books Ltd., 1979.

Thibaut, George, tr., *Vedānta Sūtras of Bādarāyaṇa with the Commentary of Śaṅkarācārya* (Two volumes), Delhi: Motilal Banarsidass, 1973.

Weber, Max, *The Religion of India*, Glencoe, Illinois: Free Press, 1958.

Williams, Monier, *Religious Thought and Life in India*, Calcutta: K.P. Bagchi & Company, 1978.

Zimmer, Heinrich, *Philosophies of India*, New York: Bollingen Foundation Inc.,1953.

Journals

The Indian Antiquary

The New Indian Antiquary, Volume of 1947, Bombay: Karthik Publishing House.

Index

adhyāsa, 80, 81, 139
Advaita, 6, 11, 16
Allen Thrasher, 31
Alvars, 33, 36
Anandagiri, 11, 23, 38
anirvacanīya, 118, 122-4
anumāna, 113-14, 117
anusandhāna, 100
arthāpatti, 113
Aryamba, 39, 40
Asiatic Researches, 2
Asvala, 58
Aurobindo, 64
avidyā, 70-1, 73-4, 76, 82, 123, 139

Bādarāyaṇa, 5, 77-80, 83, 97, 132, 135
Balavarman, 27-9
Belvalkar, 45
Bhagavad Gītā, 2, 4-6
bhakti, 6, 33, 37, 66, 99, 153-4
bhakti-yoga, 66
Bhandarkar, D.R., 20, 24, 27-8
Bhartṛhari, 28, 31
Brahma-vidyā, 39, 158
Brahma-sākṣātkāra, 86
Brahma-loka, 79
Brahma-nirvāṇa, 65
Brahmānubhava, 99, 126
Brahma-vādinī, 53
brahmacarya, 158
brāhmaṇas (as caste), 11-12, 33, 36-7, 39, 54, 56, 64, 82, 84, 142, 144-5, 148, 156
Buddhism, 35, 79

Cārvākas, 79
Charles Wilkins, 2, 63
Cheraman Perumal, 26-7, 30
Colebrooke, H.T., 2-4, 19, 25

Dara Shikoh, 1, 4
Dasgupta, S.N., 3, 18-19, 131, 139
deep-sleep state, 13, 105
deva-yāna, 79, 91, 121
Devaraja, N.K., 131
dharma, 63, 70, 84, 125
Dharmakīrti, 31
dis-embodied-ness, 90, 94
dreaming state, 13, 117, 124
Duncan Greenless, 31, 98, 151
Dvaita, 57, 90, 145

Edgerton, 63
Eugen Burnouf, 3
Frederic Rosen, 3

Gandhi, Mahatma, 64
Ganganatha Jha, 141
Gārgī, 57-60
Gauḍapāda, 11-12, 14-18, 25, 31, 40, 139
gauṇa-pratyaya, 74
George Theibaut, 6
Govinda, 11-12, 40
Govinda Bhaṭṭa, 21
gr̥hastha āśrama, 53
*guṇa*s, 64, 68

Hiltrud Rustau, 134, 157, 158
Hsuan Tsang, 19, 22-4, 35

Indian Antiquary, 19-20, 22, 26-7
Īśvara, 43, 69-70, 119, 121, 125-6

Jainism, 34
jijñāsā, 83, 85, 99
jīvan-mukta, 80, 105, 128, 142, 148
jñāna, 66, 137
jñāna-kāṇḍa, 7
jñāna-mārga, 5, 35, 125-6, 156
jñāna-yoga, 66

kaivalya, 73
*kāmya-karma*s, 75
Kāñcī, 19, 32, 33
Karl H. Potter, 31, 45, 49
karma, 48, 65-6, 75, 89, 92-3, 127, 132, 137, 145
karma-kāṇḍa, 7, 93,139
karma-mārga, 5, 125
karma-yoga, 65
Keralotpatti, 22, 26
Kr̥ṣṇa, 63-4
kṣatriya, 54, 56, 145
kṣetra, 67-9
kṣetrajña, 64, 67-9
Kumārila, 24-5, 31, 35, 114

life-stages, 145
Logan, W., 26
loka-saṁgraha, 66
Lokāyatas, 35-6, 85

Madhvācārya, 6, 23-5, 38-9
Mahābhārata, 55, 63
Mahadevan, T.M.P., 11f, 42, 98, 107-9, 125, 141, 151, 152-3
mahāvākya, 92, 135
Maitreyī, 53-5
Maṇḍana Miśra, 31, 35, 135
Māṇḍūkya Kārikā, 11, 14
Māṇḍūkya Upaniṣad, 11-13
Max Muller, 3, 19, 22, 24-5, 77
māyā, 6-7, 16, 107, 108, 121-3, 139-42
Mīmāṁsā, 4, 35, 77, 114, 132
mithyā-pratyaya, 74
mokṣa, 6, 64, 72-5, 85, 91, 93, 107, 121, 125, 128

Nagaraja Rao, P., 153-4
naiṣkarmya, 73
Naiṣkarmyasiddhi, 47
Naiyāyikas, 86
Nakamura, Hajme, 31, 77
Narasimhachar, R., 28-30
Nāthamuni, 29-30
Nayanars, 34, 36

nirvāṇa, 67
Niṣādas, 142
niṣkāma karma yoga, 65
nitya karmas, 75
nivṛtti, 65
Nyāya School, 114

Padmapāda, 39, 47, 135
Pañcapādikā, 47
pañcāyatana pūjā, 43, 153, 155
Pandey, G.C., 77
Pandey, S.L., 77
Pāṇini, 3, 88
paramahaṁsa parivrājaka, 75, 103, 146
pāramārthika satya, 119, 127, 142, 153-4
parmātman, 99
Pathak, K.B., 20-2, 27, 31
Paul Deussen, 4, 97, 132, 140
Paul Hacker, 20, 45-8
philosophy, 16
pitṛ-yāna, 79, 137
Prabhākara, 35
Prabhakar Apte, 155
Prabhavānanda Swāmī, 15
Practical Vedānta, 9, 156, 158
pradhāna, 86
prakaraṇa granthas, 45, 97-105
prasthāna trayī, 46, 48, 97, 104, 113-14, 139, 141
pratyakṣa, 113-14, 116, 132
pravṛtti, 65
prāyaścitta karmas, 75
Puligandla, R., 132, 140
Purnavarma, 19, 22-5
puruṣa, 93
puruṣottama, 64

Radhakrishnan, 9, 18, 37, 64, 80
Raghavan, 45
Raja Rammohun Roy, 19, 157
rajas, 64
Ramakrishna Mission, 8
Ramakrishna Paramahamsa, 64
Rāmānujācārya, 6
Renou Ingalls, 31
residual *karma*, 91, 146
Ṛgveda, 87-8, 137
Rudolph Roth, 3

sādhana catuṣṭaya, 84, 99, 128, 158
Saivism, 34
Śakti cult, 34
samādhi, 76, 94
samanvaya, 80
Sāṅkhya, 79, 86.
saṁnyāsa, 35, 39, 64, 125, 148
saṁnyāsin, 12, 39, 40, 158
saṁsāra, 5, 7, 66, 69, 70-2, 74, 76, 102, 118-19
Sangeku Mayeda, 45-6
Sanskrit, 3, 33, 36-7
Sarvajñātman, 28-30
śāstras, 70,114-16, 132-3
Satchidananda Murty, K, 131, 158-9
sattva, 64
Shanbag, D.N., 154-5
Śiva, 33-4
Śivaguru, 39

śravaṇa, manana, nidhidhyāsana, 54, 89-90, 95, 100, 116, 126, 129
Śṛṅgerī, 19, 48, 99, 135
sthita-prajña, 65
student, 97-101
śūdras, 1, 9, 142, 144, 148
Sundaram Pillai, P., 21

tamas, 64, 71
tattva-jñāna, 106
teacher, 97, 103, 107, 114-16, 129
Telang, K.T., 21-2, 30
Tiele, 20-1
ṭīkā, 11
Tilak, 64
Toṭakācārya, 47, 135
tyāga, 64

Uddālaka Āruṇi, 58
untouchable, 9
*upādhi*s, 118
upāsanā, 89, 127

Vaiśeṣikas, 79
Vaiṣṇava saints, 33
vaiśyas, 12, 145
Vāmadeva, 92
vānaprastha āśrama, 53
Vedānta Paribhāṣā, 113.
Vedānta Sūtras, 5, 77
Vedas, 1, 2, 39, 54, 84, 89, 93, 115, 126, 145
Venkateswaran, S.V., 29, 30
vidyā, 82
Vidyāraṇya, 38
Viṣṇu, 33
Vivekānanda, Swāmī, 8-9, 156, 158
Vyāsa, 41
vyāvahārika satya, 99, 119, 120, 126, 127, 142, 153

waking state, 13, 105, 125
Weber, 25
William Jones, 2

Yājñavalkya, 53-9, 93, 116, 149
yoga, 64- 7